# ONIONS

# AND

# ARTICHOKES

*Understanding the Deepest*

*Layers Within,*

*A Recipe For Authentic Joy*

# TABLE OF CONTENTS

# Chapter One

## The Arete Process

The ancient Greeks used the word "arete" [ahr-i-tey] to imply excellence cultivated through harnessing the essence — the inherent quality — of the entity itself. Since all that exists possesses its own essence, and thus, its own unique potential for excellence, the implication of the word would change depending on the point of focus. For instance, the arete of a rose is distinct from that of a tulip. I'm sure you would agree that the arete of the human experience is one that resonates within the higher spectrum of emotional energy, like joy, exuberance, and even, peace. The process described in this book epitomizes the original use of the word, arete, because it intends to both penetrate and summon forth qualities existing within your highly complex yet, pure and concise, elixir of "beingness". Your own excellence is only relative to the proximity of who you are being in thought, emotion, and action with who you authentically are, not necessarily in compliance with, or relative to, the idealized constructs of society, family, or culture.

The most important thing to know is that self-love is the only doorway through which your authenticity can be set free. Thus, the Arete Process is designed with three specific intentions, the overall of which is to be your architect in creating this doorway. The first is to integrate all aspects of your being for the purpose of returning to wholeness, which you will experience as genuine happiness. That is, to assist the integration of the personal, relational, and supra-personal sides of your nature, so that you can tap into the inherent strength and nature of your being. This integration is the engine that generates inspired action and the actualization of your potential. With such guidance you will reclaim aspects of yourself that you have been unconsciously suppressing. This is only important because suppression is what leads to excessive depression, anxiety, frustration, anger and, eventually, physical ailments. The real solution to the insecurity regarding certain areas of your life, whether it be romantic relations, friendships, money, health, or career, is to develop a secure relationship with yourself. This is done by seeing into the depths of you and by loving all of the layers within — the positive and the seemingly negative.

The other two intentions of the Arete Process as a strategy are for you to avoid specific pot-holes that I had fallen into along my path of transformation, in the hopes that you will not do the same. The first is the trap of using spirituality as a guise or a tool to remain in a state of denial and pseudo-self love. Only after we fully embrace our humanity can we detach from our construct of self all together, but never before. Using spirituality as a means to bypass your real-world day to day, or emotional issues is a brilliant disguise in its own right, yet it is just a disguise that eventually leads to greater suffering.

The second pothole I wish for you to avoid is that of attempting to supersede the human process of learning and integration. Although some specific action is required, the Arete Process is not necessarily only a step-by-step process of *doing*, of actions to take per se, in and of itself. Rather, it is designed, by exposing you to new perspectives, to initiate your own insights in a way that will help you assimilate this information on all levels of your being — intellectually, physically, and of course, emotionally. Knowledge cannot lead to transformation if it remains at a cognitive level alone. It must become an embodied part of your reality for it to influence your perception, and positive or effective action. It must become a composite of your subconscious to alter your perception of reality. Significant shifts becomes personalized and normalized through emotional involvement.

Essentially, this is a guided journey of personal transformation through an integrative process involving emotional transmutations and perceptual alterations — from those that stem from self-hate to those that embody self-love. Such guidance comes not from the perspective of a trained psychologist or an enlightened guru, rather from the personal experience and perspective of an ordinary woman who ventured with perseverance into her past and highly probable future in order to understand her suffering — until specific truths were revealed and joy became fully embodied.

Although my suggestion that your starting point may be that of self-hate may seem extreme, and frankly, quite grim, all self-induced suffering is a result of not seeing the truth of you, and thus rejecting certain aspects of yourself. You will soon discover that habitual emotional patterns ranging from anguish to anxiety result from not loving yourself. Among other positive experiences, what emerges from self-love is authenticity. Aside from feeling comfortable in your own skin, comes a underlying sense of fulfillment, genuine connection to humanity, and greater appreciation for life itself.

While, as a result of integrating this information you will eventually discontinue recreating the unwanted conditions that you currently perpetuate, my intention is not to guide you into the same never ending chase for perfection you are likely very familiar with. If it were, I'd be of no service to you. Nevertheless, I do understand that when the world shows us evidence that is the opposite of who we deep down know ourselves to be, we feel intense discomfort. This perceived discrepancy often evokes feelings of hopelessness and restriction, as if grounded industrial-grade chains are wrapped around our ankles preventing our flourishing. Aligning with your truth requires that you acknowledge the real composition of the "chains" keeping you stuck and the real composition of yourself. What you assume is the source of your restriction is not. Rather, it is what currently resides below your level of awareness. True self-awareness is the only thing required for you to see what is or isn't already here. Your shadow consists of the aspects of your higher mind and your conditioned personality inclusive of desires and fears, and experiences existing deep within, but outside your conscious awareness. It is only after you shed light upon the *influential* aspects of your shadow that you can then realize that there are no chains. This realization in turn, is when your illusory restrictions become the structure that allows the doorway to freedom to exist. The illusions themselves become the precise catalysts to self-love.

# A Journey Through Emotional
## Transmutations and Perceptual Alterations

The two most important points I can make are that *whatever you assume is true becomes what the universe is invited to confirm in your reality, and whatever aspects of you that are part of you — your personality and unresolved emotional experiences — that you push away from you also become what the universe is invited to confirm in your reality.* Your universe, no matter how far removed from how you wish it were, is none other than a subjective paradigm of reality, or point of awareness. Which potential reality you align with is brought forth through your most consistent beliefs and emotions — your underlying state of being, and your elixir of resolved and unresolved experiences. It is through these projections that you are accessing various dimensions of possibility.

In your temporal experience, once you identify yourself with a belief, it evolves into an inextricable part of you — you and it become one and the same, and so do your conditional circumstances. In general, as you shift your beliefs about yourself and the world to those that serve you, you experience the version of yourself consistent with your desired parallel reality. This being only part of the equation though. More relevant for your awakening and integration is to understand where the non-serving beliefs stem from. It is the unprocessed life experiences that have the greatest influence upon your belief structure. Recognition of these experiences offers the access points in which resolutions can take place. Unprocessed life-experiences are crucial because of the disassociation within you that takes place as a result. When we experience situations that cannot be resolved in our early life we have to disassociate from them. We have to separate from them and our consciousness splits. Our sense of self fragments resulting in multiple internal selves, some of which we burry into our subconscious. With this, we stop relating to them and we then lose our compassion for them altogether. This rejection, lack of compassion, and understanding is precisely the source of our anxiety and inner-conflict. Furthermore, each of these aspects of you have their own beliefs. You are only aware of the ones you have not rejected, yet the ones you've suppressed are still influencing your choices and life experiences. The world is always reflecting back to us what is really going on inside of us. This is why self-love is the most important underlying state of being for all of humanity. Self-love as a process involves re-integrating these split off aspects of yourself through the venue of compassion.

Sometimes, for some of us, attaining this state requires a bit of work, which is why I refer to it as a process. The "work", paradoxically, involves both an element of letting go of the self completely and an element of complete inquisitive self-absorption. That is, a letting go of our very own self-image which we have constructed out of self-preservation efforts — with all of their psychological distortions and pathological attachments, fears and anxieties — to pierce through and get a glimpse of what is underneath it all. But, in order to do this, first must come a deep inquiry into those very same constructs. This is how you shed the heavy layers of self-doubt and confusion that cover your authenticity.

Once you realize that much of your personal identity began as an intelligent survival strategy stemming from a limited understanding of the dynamics at play within your immediate environment, you can begin to see its illusions.

Many of us unconsciously split off from our inherent natural expressions of self and construct other ones — others that we assume are necessary for our advancement or safety. We do this many, many times throughout our life. The problem though is that these same unconscious strategies eventually and inevitably become a source of inner conflict. They often block our growth and become obstructions simply because they are no longer necessary and they are not expressions of our authentic nature. They are facades that feel like striving and are nothing more than fear based self-image attachments at their core.

In resolving this, sometimes an emotional resolution — a healing shift in your cellular memory and emotional body — is necessary. As these experiences become resolved and you tap into your larger nature, your ego and many of its defense mechanisms cease to be the master of your choices. First, acknowledging each of these aspects of your personality as valid is a must. Validating them requires that you understand how, and have compassion for why, they developed in the first place, not by continuing to reject them. At times, recognizing the inherent intelligence of your personality "project" is all that is required. Your true nature will no longer be overshadowed by beliefs originally born out of self-protection and self-rejection that over time had hardened into what seems to be a permanent way of being. With this in mind, the initial phase of this journey essentially requires a deep dive into the inception of the very same constructs that had caused your truth to be forgotten in the first place by consciously delving into them to uncover their deeper intent. Their deeper intent can then be redirected in powerful life-affirming ways.

I can tell you with complete certainty that, ultimately, living in a state of inauthenticity is the source of our struggle and emotional suffering. Anything that feels as though it breathes more life into your experience is an indication that you are aligning with your authenticity, but often what comes first feels like nothing short of suffocation.

While both my spiritual seeking and interest in psycho therapeutic practices were originally motivated by relief from myself, eventually I understood that the eagerness to escape myself was precisely the engine giving exponential power to my struggle. Whatever problem or struggle you are faced with — even the most stubborn and infectious — when you develop a relationship with it, it becomes the path of liberation.

*** 

Much of this guidance toward greater self-love can be simplified and described as an integration of three western psychological processes — the Focusing method, Inner Child work, and Shadow work — coupled with spiritual principles drawn upon form the East — specifically that the Mahayana and Tantric schools of Buddhism, and Buddhist Psychology. While I do not get into much detail regarding these three areas of spiritual doctrine, I do point to some of its primary philosophies simply because they offer perspectives based upon universal truths and the essence of humanity. Such guidance serves to evoke both self-actualization (creating a life that expresses and utilizes your potential and purpose) and self-realization (recognizing higher degrees of your spiritual nature). Self-realization enhances these psychological processes, and these psychological processes, in turn, will enhance your spiritual understanding and devotion. As a disclaimer: while this book offers descriptions of emotional healing modalities, seeing a qualified professional is my absolute recommendation if necessary.

In short, the Focusing method offers a felt experience of self-love in the moments of your greatest challenges. It brings you squarely face to face with your personal experience of mind, emotion and physiology as it all occurs. Inner Child work, on the other hand, is an expression of loving yourself in the past — precisely where you had experienced love and security as lacking. That is, where love was not present in any external physical form with you (in your perception at the time). Shadow work utilizes what you are perceiving as outside yourself as a tool to see what is within. It also gets to the heart of the dominant dynamics within the construct of your most important relationships. As a byproduct, Shadow work evokes compassion for others by causing you to recognize yourself in others.

Genuine self-love is also necessary for realizing the supra-personal (universal) aspect of your nature without convoluting it with your original coping mechanisms. Pseudo self-love leaves the door wide open for greater self-rejection under the guise of spirituality. From a place of greater balance you can come to know experientially that your personality, your emotions, your perceptions, your beliefs, and your physical body are ultimately an illusionary boundary of self-definition produced out of the fear of non-existence. With this understanding you will recognize that you are one with the source of all creation, and as such, are eternal and unconditionally loved by something larger. Thus, you are worthy of the most abundant and joyful experience of life possible.

# What Brought Me Here:
## The Rise of Self-Love

I happened to be part of two families whose life-styles and values were at complete opposite ends of the spectrum. On one end, my family's exemplifications of reality succumbed to alcoholism, depression, rage, verbal abuse, extreme pessimism, excessive fear, and addiction as normal, and on the other end, my family's exemplification of reality asserted kindness, constructive conflict resolution, physical health, success, and happiness. While my home life with my mother was fraught with the kind of dysfunction common to alcoholic homes, my home life with my father offered stability and belonging. Yet, I chose to be with my mother more. I mention this polarity because I think that my experience with these two very different perspectives is what has allowed me to observe each objectively; I had something to compare each to. An objective perspective is what allowed me to dissect its various dynamics and intricacies.

I can only speculate what may be the source of my mom's dysfunction. In short, my mom's father, Snooks Gordon, was an extremely successful businessman and famous Golden Gloves boxer in Peoria, Illinois in the 30's and 40's. My mother's young life was one of physical comfort and luxury, but right around the time I was born she experienced a life altering event that to this day has not been processed and dealt with in any constructive capacity. In her early thirties her father passed and her brother convinced her that it would be best if he handled the fortune that their father had left for them. Her brother then was involved in several bad investments and lost all of my mother's security. First went the cash, then the assets inclusive of their homes and businesses. Point being that she, in a matter of about two years, went from extreme wealth to extreme poverty, and didn't know how to tap into her inner resources to resolve this dilemma. I was born right into her dynamic of extreme despair, anger, regret, and learned helplessness. I remained with her as she descended into greater and greater depression, and addiction as her way of coping with this difficult and unexpected transition.

The results of my ensuing distraught home-life included disorganized attachment and post traumatic stress disorder, and my dedication to finding contentment and joy had resulted in the unraveling of these effects. Nevertheless, you do not have to have had an excessively difficult childhood in order to benefit from what I have to offer here. While this book does place attention upon this as a cause of certain emotional challenges, we as a collective part of humanity all struggle with similar effects. Particularly, our western culture, simply because we were never taught how to use our emotions as a guidances system. Instead we were taught that our emotions are insignificant and we should simply get rid of them all together, hence my mother's addictions and the booming pharmaceutical pandemic as an integral part of our modern western culture.

Positive reinforcement, admiration, encouragement, security, and the like offers life-affirming parenting that feeds the emergence of things like confidence and self-esteem in children. Without which, these same children, as adults, remain in a sort of arrested development — unsure of how to tap into adaptive natural human qualities. Essentially, a dysfunctional family life being the foundation from which I was trying to create a joyful life as a young adult, wasn't working very well for me. Part of my struggle was due to the fact that I am extremely sensitive and highly empathic. As a result, I had created a bubble of separation from myself and others simply because I did not understand these sensitivities. This led to debilitating anxiety, broken relationships, and panic attacks. Needless to say, I was very unhappy, very lonely, and very scared for many years. Due to my isolation I became extremely paranoid and began having delusions that people were following me. Feeling, for the most part, extremely vulnerable, lost and unloved, if people did offer expressions of love to me I couldn't see it.

It wasn't until the energy it took to remain in a state of self-deprivation had exceeded what my physical body was capable of that I began seeking external counsel to improve my life. Anorexia was the very first catalysts for me. Seeing others' reaction to my physical appearance forced me to open my eyes and I started becoming more aware of my behavior, perceptions and negative emotions. Eventually I learned that memorized within all dimensions of my being was a plethora of suppressed unresolved trauma that needed my attention.

Although some of the given advice at the time was educated, it often lacked wisdom. Both friendly and professional suggestions, while true in their own right, were too far out of reach form me, so remained idealogical. Advice like, just listen to my heart or to just change my thoughts only exacerbated my confusion. I had never cultivated a positive sense of self-trust, so how could I listen to my heart? The communication stream from my heart to my mind was way too convoluted with layers of unresolved experiences to hear an utterance, much less understand it. Even more than this, to change my thoughts seemed impossible because I didn't know which ones needed to change. If my thoughts both validated and created my perception of reality, how could I possibly be discretionary, and how could I possibly un-believe them?

Looking back, at the time I was only capable of oscillating between unconsciously giving myself more of what was most familiar, and simultaneously, consciously striving with desperate attempts at avoiding this familiarity because it brought me intense feeling of shame. Confusion and chaos continued to dominate my life until I found my first true inkling of hope in universal axioms. Upon learning that even chaos has its own kind of order that is impossible to comprehend from an assumed linear perspective of which humanity is most familiar, I realized that I needed to see things differently. My perspective needed to change before I could comprehend the inherent order of my life. It was the unseen that I had to acknowledge before any of my positive efforts would bear fruit. I learned that by shedding light upon the imperceptible and ineffable from both a very myopic and a more expanded perspective, my life could be transformed.

As a result of my distrust in others, universal principles became the compass that guided me to my highest personal truth, paradoxically beyond the self. Yet, for a period of time, these principles became a vehicle with which I bypassed my life challenges — like that of not trusting others. I'll get to the topic of spiritual bypassing in an upcoming chapter. I eventually did come to realize that there exists a powerfully synergistic relationship among universal fundamental truths of existence and our deeply subjective truths. Ignoring one in favor of the other often leads to emotional and psychological imbalances that effect our day to day life within the realms of family, career, money, etc. In actuality, universal fundamental truths of existence and our deeply subjective truths are complementary and depend on each other to experience their own essence.

Because we all must find a way to met our needs, I turned to spirituality for support that was not present in physical form and to meet my need for connection and love, and toward psychology in search of healing. With that said, I spent years developing a certain level of genuine spiritual insight, beginning with my Hatha Yoga practice and mediation, and into intellectual study of both the Bhagavad Gita and the Buddhist doctrine. Despite this, I remained stuck in habitual patterns that did not serve to enhance my life experience and continued to create very uncomfortable dynamics for myself, specifically in my career, and in my relationships. This challenged my faith of course, but fortunately never hindered my devotion.

I remained persistent in trying to understand this dilemma, or seeming contradiction. This inspired inquiry into teachings of modern popular coaches like Tony Robbins, and spiritual teachers like Betinho Massaro and Teal Swan. While it may seem from the outside that their philosophies are rooted in pop-psychology, they provide a wealth of wisdom of which I have no words to express my degree of appreciation for. These leaders are bringing an integration of psychotherapeutic methods and spiritual insight to the mainstream society… precisely where it belongs. Nevertheless, it is one thing to listen to these teachings and another to actually apply them and integrate them within your own paradigm of reality.

The most significant scientific discoveries point

to evidence that we are one with the source of all that is. We are each an integral part of the fabric of creation we may call Source Energy or Cosmic Consciousness. Because we are all an extension of God, we are God, and thus, we are the creators and the created. It is those who have assumed themselves to be separate from this source of existence itself that believe that they are unworthy. It is these people who have the most to offer others when they realize the truth of their inseparability with Source. Their personal experience allows for a greater understanding of the majority of the western population that shares the self-sentiment that they are not enough, good enough, or worthy enough to be loved by "the universe" when in fact they are an extension of it. Internal freedom is birthed by a specific kind of knowing: one of undeniable self-worth coupled with courageous self-trust and a resolute faith that the universe has your back.

Unawareness of your inextricable existence with the source of creation itself, is one reason why it is so hard to love ourselves. Another is because the mind happens to be brilliant at its own deception. It can convince a starving person that he or she is not. In fact, it can convince this same person that they are overweight and excessively gluttonous. This deceptive workings of the mind can be observed with one of the most obvious examples of which I am personally far too familiar with — anorexia.

Self-deprivation is a state of constriction caused by excessive feelings of shame. It is not virtuous to reject and repress yourself, as some people in your life may have convinced you to believe. Self-expression is part of your purpose for existing in the first place. The opposite of which is to restrict the flow of source energy through you. Choosing to hide ourselves from others, and often from ourselves, gives us a sense of control, it causes us to feel safe, but can only lead to problems because it defies our very purpose for coming into this physical life experience. Your own form of self-deprivation may not be that of "malnourishment" reflected in your physical appearance and health, but it may be reflected in your career, your relationship with money, to joy and fun, to connections and friendships, to spiritual depth and understanding, to intellectual value, to your physical environment, or to romantic relationship.

Everything is given to you by you to teach you something that serves your growth, even your own mind's deceptions. This is one reason why the subjective truths of what is objective reality for some people contradict those for others depending on what is needed for their own personal expansion. When you see your greatest "issue" as serving your highest good and you actually discover what that is, your relationship with it becomes positive and it ceases to exist as an obstacle to your fulfillment. Once the wound heals in your cellular memory, the unconscious data supporting its negative charge is replaced with new data that is intentional. This is creation.

In many cases, your pain is calling for you to recognize something important and necessary; it is inviting you to awaken, to change in some way and heal wounds from your past. However it manifests for you is the necessary condition to bring forth the specific cellular memory you are needing to acknowledge and then clear out. Once we attend to our feelings and the original occurrence that ignited them, the new clarity accommodates a shift in your perspective.

My encouragement to intentionally reflect upon your emotional pain is not an invitation for self-pity. Rather, it is an invitation for your awakening, from which clarity and true empowerment will prevail. You will learn that once the causation of your self-defeating patterns  are attended to properly, you are no longer a "victim" to them. They were created by you to serve you in some powerful way — you cannot be a victim to your own creation. They are actually here to be used as catalysts to catapult your life forward, as perhaps you had originally intended.

You will see that the dark and the light are necessary components to your expansion; that without the dark you would not have access to the warmest, brightest, and purest depths of the divine source of all existence. This is why I can say with confidence that eventually you will be grateful for the very challenge or pain that brought you to this here in the first place.

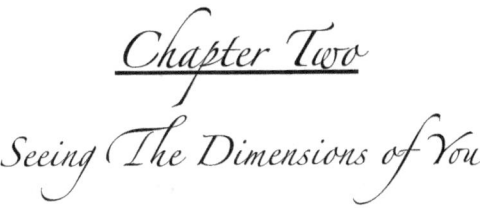

# Chapter Two

## Seeing The Dimensions of You

Consider how each leaf of an artichoke has two sides; while the deeper leaves remain entirely hidden from sunlight, the outermost leaves have a side that is exposed and a side that is not. The inner unexposed side of each artichoke leaf is where the substance is. This is true for you and me as well. Each individual aspect of our personality has an exposed side and a shadow side. It is within the shadow aspects that the "meat" of our being resides. The sides of us that we reject and deny, that is.

Each learned aspect of your personality, as well as each fear and ambition you've grown attached to, has embedded within a depth of experience that remains hidden from your conscious awareness. It is these experiences that have the greatest impact upon the unfolding of your life experience. When the experiences and feelings contained within your cellular memory are summoned forth with the intention to be resolved they unlock profound healing. Just as the layered leaves of an artichoke offer an unexpected treasury of nutrition, each of the layers of you offer such in the form of insight, release, and inspiration. By attending to these occurrences with more compassionate validation, you can choose to either allow the layers of your personality they had resulted in to be fluid and flexible, present or absent, or you may choose to re-design them with completely new intentions.

Like that of the artichoke, there are also layers upon layers of our being that enclose and protect our heart. The outermost layers of you, those you have been taught are "good" are what you show to the world....and to yourself. These are the masks you wear. From your appraisal of how well you live up to each mask you gain a sense of self-worth, or lack thereof, accordingly. Those that you were taught were wrong are the ones you shove away. You cannot actually get rid of what is a part of you so you must relocate the awareness of them to your subconscious. The problem with this is that your truth always shows up, but in this case in covert manipulative ways. This then causes a greater split within because part of you knows when you are doing this. The first step toward authenticity therefore, is to courageously acknowledge what you really feel, whether that is what society (and you) deems as good, or not. Then become introspective enough to see why you feel this way.

For instance, if you feel anger toward someone rather than deny that feeling, allow it to be by sinking into it and then ask it where it is coming from. Ask why is it here? It has something to say. What need is it trying to fulfill? It is holding a specific truth of experience that needs to be addressed. Knowing that anger or rage is not a productive long-term state of being you will know that there is something that needs to be resolved.

I've often seen people that take out their anger on innocent people simply because it had been so suppressed that it had to find a way out. They find a way out but unfortunately, outside the context of the actual situation that has caused it to begin with because they are afraid, or don't know how, to express it within the context in which it belongs.

This is the patron of a store who rages at the associate and displays a child-like temper tantrum for a minor slight or irritation. If you look for it, you will see this behavior everywhere. Perhaps you have been the person reacting this way, I know I have. You'll soon realize that this type of reaction is a result of suppressing the truth of our experience, as opposed to addressing it directly and constructively. It is a result of certain needs not being met constructively. It is an indication that there are concerns that are not being expressed and handled directly, and there are wounds that have not healed within us. This negligence culminates into reactions that seem out of context. Clearly, living inauthentically is extremely volatile and causes incredible anxiety.

If there is something that is a part of you and that is among your authentic needs, you can meet those needs directly as opposed to doing so in manipulative ways. For instance, you may need to feel as sense of protection because you actually feel vulnerable in the world. If you are suppressing this need, you may only show to the world a strong empowered being. You will likely even physically be strong relative to societies norm. But because you suppress your desire and need to feel protected, you generate dynamics that threaten your survival or safety so that you can get the need met. Simply stated, until we acknowledge who we really are behind the masks, we continue to play out familiar stories. We remain uncomfortable in our own skin…and in our own home, and in our career, and in our family, the list goes on.

The layers of truth closest to our heart are the most elusive to your conscious awareness *and* the most significant in regards to the unfolding of our potential. These deeper layers contain wisdom that has the power to unhook the chains, or release the emotional anchors, currently keeping you contained within unwanted conditions or emotional patterns. Rejection of these deepest layers within you only strengthens their grip upon your heart — restricting the natural flow of life into your experience. And with rejection as your recourse, it is only possible to find yourself continuing to strive for freedom, but forever falling short.

This creates a war within ourselves that strengthens precisely the parts of our personalty we are trying to push away and perpetuates patterns of discord in certain areas of our life. Even though at this point, this fact may seem irrelevant I can assure you that self-rejection is precisely why you have, in so many ways, tried to overcome but to no avail, continue to re-create evidence of the same unwanted pattern once again.

I suspect that you have experienced times when you had tried with incredible will-power to change a certain condition in your life, but instead of creating what you had hoped for, you remained right where you started. This is equivalent to trying to toast bread without the toaster plugged in. You go through all of the motions of placing the bread in the slots, adjusting the toaster to the desired level of toasting, then pushing the lever down. But nothing happens if it's not plugged in. The same is true for you.

If you are not "plugged in" to beliefs and emotions that are in harmony with your desired outcome, you will not get the results you are consciously applying so much effort toward achieving. This can be very subtle sometimes because a core belief is one that you may not realize you have, nevertheless, it is dictating your results. It reflects an accumulation of the thought patterns you have had for so many years that they are just immediate and automatic. For many of us, these core beliefs contradict our true aspirations and authenticity.

It is only after facing toward and loving these split off aspects of you that effective resolution of our negative memories can take place, and with this, the specific patterns they produce in your life can cease to be. This is when you will have integrated the truth of you, and as a result the reflection in the mirror will change.

Acknowledging the deeper layers within you allows them to release their need to protect your heart. Your emotions and each aspect of you must be validated and loved first. This is how they will become reintegrated. This is when the most hidden, densest, and darkest layers can expand and open to the penetrating warmth of the sunlight. It is in this release that your freedom resides. With each layer's incremental and gracious liberation from hiding, the magnetic force that is pulling you toward your most inspired and joyful self actually succeeds at bringing you closer.

Before we uncover what we have suppressed, what we see is only the surface — the end product. And then we try to change our conditioning — our karma — (or habitual ways of thinking, believing, and perceiving in our efforts to maintain a sense of self, relative permanence and certainty) from that superficial perspective. This is akin to trying to change your reflection in the mirror by manipulating the reflection itself. It's simply impossible, yet you continue to observe yourself struggling to change it. True change comes from within — never from surface manipulation.

No doubt that a deeper awareness of yourself and a broader understanding that will push against some ideas you have been adhering to but are not serving you. With this I hope to evoke your own realization that you can question the cognitive plane that you have built your life upon. Instead of continuing to believe what does not serve your well-being, I invite you to see the world differently. Without knowing your actual capacity to create your life, it appears chaotic and unsafe because it is consumed by a different level of mind – one where survival is its sole concern.

What must come after you realize that you have a choice in all of this is the release of mental and emotional anchors that are ultimately keeping you from where you want to go. Until these are released, you may read or listen to the wisest and most profound content, but your life will remain unchanged, or at best, it will change very slowly. The resistance that keeps this information from penetrating all dimensions of you is a specific genre of core beliefs that completely contradict the fundamental truths of existence. Therefore, to release the resistance is to actively address what you are assuming about the world and yourself — but first only relative to actual truths of existence. With this you will be able to see their inaccuracy. Fundamental truths offer the only objective platform of accurate comparison, all else is subjective and therefore forever evasive.

We are not here to conform, which is precisely why it is impossible to obey the standards and expectations of everyone at all times. The only possibility is to comply with your own standards and expectations of yourself while maintaining a high degree of integrity. Seeing that all else is an illusion contained only within the subjectivity of random personal inferences will also allow you to glimpse your entire life from a perspective that is closer to that of the source of existence itself.

As more and more anchors are released, your baseline state of being naturally elevates, your awareness expands, and you become more receptive to higher perspectives that then offer one transformation after another. Your own shifts in perspective invariably cause a shift in your expectations and actions and, thus, your conditions change without aggressive force. Your past experiences can be observed from the highest truth which only you can discover for yourself. Nobody can tell you what this is. Only you can tap into this wisdom because it is your own.

# Chapter Three

## A Broader and Higher Awareness

I invite you to think of your authentic self as the detached observer of your thoughts, your emotions, and perceptions. The act of being aware assumes that there is another level of being — one that is aware and one that is not; one that is conscious and one that is not; one that is intentional and one that is automatic. Once you bring awareness to what once was automatic, it can become intentional, you can then choose to re-live it or not. Extrapolation from familiarity requires that you choose an alternative; this requires your intention. It is intention that drives your authentic self, and unawareness that drives the conditioned self. The awareness itself is your authentic self.

Your conditioned self consists of a complex interplay of judgments and associations concerning things, people, and experiences. This is a byproduct of your ego. Inclusive to this is your mental construct of yourself relative to and separate from others (all of this existing in tandem for the assumed purpose of your physical survival). This ego-driven way of seeing the world keeps you living in the past and separate from others.

Although it's possible for the higher conscious creative mind to become the leader of our actions while the subconscious manages all of the necessities of our physical survival, as a collective we have become entirely dependent upon it regarding all aspects of our lives, even where its exclusive involvement is not needed. When you do not decide who you want to be, how you want to feel, and what you want to experience, your ego structure that is like autopilot for an airplane takes charge. The problem is that the only thing it knows by default is what can be taken from your past experiences and beliefs. Meanwhile, we are here to direct creation in the deliberate unfolding of our singular point of consciousness, which is a necessary part of the whole.

The cultivation of self-awareness is your road to freedom. It is not by accident that we have the ability to be aware of how we are choosing to perceive things and that we can choose otherwise. This ability, called metacognition, (a function of the prefrontal cortex) can be cultivated through the practice of meditation. The enhancement of this function eventually changes the way your brain works by activating the neocortical regions in completely new ways. Through the practice of meditation and mindful investigation you can begin to catch yourself before going unconscious. You can see your emotional addictions, in feeling and in action, and in effect choose to disengage the old redundant neural-networks so that new ones form.

Higher perspective, the ability to see the truth regarding each and every circumstance, unrestricted by our conditioning, is only possible with wholeness of self. The more integrated we become the higher our perspective reaches. That is, the more we love the aspects of ourself we once rejected and the more we embrace the feelings we once ignored, the more integrated we become, and thus, the more conscious our choices will be. Additionally, with conscious choice of actions, thoughts, and beliefs, the better you will feel and the more you will align with your desired life experiences.

As I insinuated previously, for some of us, it is first through positively identifying with the self, that we can then detach from our identity all together. Your true joy and peace will emerge when you detached from the masks designed by your ego, with this, they are no longer in control of you. You see them as optional and choose any of them as you wish. This, in turn, automatically provokes questions regarding who you really are and what your purpose for existing is. You will begin to know that your true being is not you thoughts, not your emotions, not you beliefs, and not your body. What is left is simply awareness and consciousness — one with the source of all existence.

# Your Inseparability With The Source of All Existence

If you were receptive to the previous content of this book, your own integration of the very first phase has already begun and will continue to unfold throughout the book. The most important aspect of this process is for you to realize your profound value exactly as you are. In knowing that you are an expression of Source, you cannot deny your significance and value. My goal is for you to allow this truth becomes the foundation upon which your new construct of reality is built.

Owning the truth that you are one with cosmic consciousness, and thus, an inseparable part of the infinite field of possibility, establishes a very important foundation. That being that you are inherently worthy, despite externally and internally superimposed assumptions of what defines worthiness. Knowing that at your core you are one with the source of all existence automatically dissolves the fears that keep you from loving all parts to you. Fear is the only emotion that keeps you resisting all aspects of your true personality.

Like our personal expansion, universal expansion is never a done deal either because it is an expression of infinite possibilities through ever present energy guided by our free-will and being realized through awareness and experience. It is important to understand that energy within the human experience does not have a will of its own, it is itself neutral and dependent on our consciousness. That is, our assumed projection or expectation of it is what defines it as such. The energy itself is the source from which all that we perceive with our senses is birthed, but is not separate from our consciousness. Energy exists to be shaped by the agency of your free will. Your experience is therefore designed by you.

Quantum theory shows consistent evidence of life being a part of a holographic universe. Cosmology shows us evidence that all that we observe in outer space does not actually exist now. What we are witnessing in the now is that of billions of years in the past. Neuroscience shows us that what we observe with our senses, while we believe is out there in space, is taken into our cognitive awareness via microscopic receptors within and on our bodies. Quantum physics shows us that the particle is only a wave of probability, of potential, until it is observed. Our observation makes it what it exist as matter. How could that be?

Additionally, quantum physics proves to us that all is here and now, forever and always. Within the framework of this truth is that all relevant potential realities are possible because all are present simultaneously here and now. Potential is what you have already been realizing into your experience. "Quantum physicists now know that we are all part of a field of energy that contains all possibilities and never ceases to exist, it only changes form in physical reality where time and space exist," says Dr. Joe Dispenza, author of *Breaking The Habit of Being Yourself* and a researcher who explores the science behind spontaneous remissions (how people heal themselves of chronic conditions and terminal diseases). All that will ever exists already infinitely exists within the field of infinite potential which, I reference to as the function of "Source Energy". Our experience is our reality and we have never experienced something outside of our own consciousness. You can choose your point of view of the same one thing anytime you wish, which then collapses a different reality into your experience accordingly.

Subatomic particles do not collapse into a perceivable experience or physical form (a particle) until observed. It is the observation, the expectation, the point of conscious awareness, that is required for it to become some "thing" other than potential energy. The observer affects the behavior of energy and matter in this way, which is why it is termed the observer effect. "With this discovery, mind and matter can no longer be considered separate; they are intrinsically related because the subjective mind produces measurable changes on the objective physical world," says Dr. Dispenza. In other words, the energy of any potential reality, as if it were already in existence, responds to our thoughts and feelings and therefore is what gives it form.

We are always attracting into our life what we

are emotionally resonant with. That is, both our current surface level state of being, and our previous unintegrated (emotionally unresolved) aspects of self dictate our experience of reality. I encourage you to recognize the significance of this. We have just been under a false assumption — that our conditions are what determines our experience — when in fact, it is the other way around. Chosen from the pool of infinite potential realities, you are collapsing certain relevant configurations of "reality" into your projection — into your awareness of an experience. In truth, you are generating your experience and placing it onto everything that you perceive as outside yourself. What this means is that you are the perceiver and what you are perceiving.

Waiting upon the universe to deliver or create what you want is a thoroughly ineffective approach yet, summoning its presence within you, and through you, as part of you, is necessary and highly effective. Increased awareness offers a transition from believing that all you see and experience with your senses and your emotions is externally forced upon you, to the awareness of being the generator of all that you experience — assume, feel, and see. With this awareness it becomes clear that choosing the perspective that makes you feel good is the most effective use of your consciousness.

In upcoming chapters I will remind you of your ability to alchemize your negative emotional past and teach you the science behind cultivating authentic positivity in the present so that you can effectively shift your state of being and expose yourself to a whole new domain of possibility. But first we must attend to some deeper aspects of you — resolve your emotional wounds and reclaim your shadow aspects of self — to establish wholeness. This is what is meant by, integration.

# Chapter Four

## The Dichotomy of Emotion: When We Cannot Hear The Still Voice Within

Paradoxically, a methodical hyper-awareness of yourself as encouraged with this process will eventually lead you to a "divine" release from, or non-attachment to, definitions of yourself. Efforts, whether conscious or unconscious, to prove ourselves or to defend our self-image in any particular way, consumes a lot of energy; energy that could be extended outward in ways that benefit others. You will, in time, come to a place where you just know that ultimately, the thoughts and emotions that construct your personality are all optional and that engaging in them is a moment by moment choice. This paradoxical state which oscillates between acute self-awareness and non-attachment is supported by the sense of a subtle, but extremely positive surrendering to the universe. With this your energy is then no longer consumed by striving to maintain who you think you are or should be, and thus, more of yourself can be given. Your definition of success shifts to how efficiently and abundantly giving flows through you in service of humanity.

A very common source of anxiety for most

people is the perpetual re-creation of a self-image — one in which you need to constantly uphold and protect. This self-image preservation becomes a primary motivation behind your choices and actions, and thus, your efforts are not always pure. Obviously when this is the case, we make choices that do not actually serve our overall wellbeing, because we are at the whim of others. We are doing things and being certain ways to appease others and to gain approval. Our vision and intention becomes convoluted without even our conscious awareness for the most part, which is, in turn, the source of another common undertow of anxiety we are constantly feeling. This is why Buddhist theory and practice offers significant release of tension. It reconnects us with our authentic nature in many ways because it evokes the realization.

Acknowledging this ultimate truth — that our thoughts, beliefs, and feelings are all illusions of a self — releases resistance, which emerges in the forms of attachments and cravings. Attachment to these illusions introduces resistance to the flow of positive abundant life-energy into our experience. Recognizing the incessant oscillation between craving and avoiding always present and motivating our actions within our human nature is the first step to releasing this very tendency.

Our emotional experiences and cognitive constructs begin with fundamental illusions inherent to our five senses. Our senses are no more than filtering mechanisms through which we experience "reality". For example, our hearing is only within a specific limited vibrational range. Any sound outside of this range remains non-existent to you, they nevertheless do exist. Not only this, every present moment is in truth a past moment. What occurs to you as now is in fact from nanoseconds prior to. Also, the effects that our beliefs can have upon our physical body is profound. Our beliefs can transform our body, they can cure cancer, and they can cause our death. Our beliefs are part of the matrix of illusion and self-deception in which we live and experience as reality.

Even our personality is nothing more than a construct based upon our accumulated experiences. There is something within each of us that is true, that is timeless and unwavering. It is at the center of you, below all the layers of your ego construct. This is our deeper self, our core, our heart, our higher self — that which recognizes itself as one with the source of all existence. Our truth is sometimes brought forth through a knowing, or a very subtle voice from within.

As mentioned previously, we consist of three inter-dynamic dimensions, including our emotional body, our cognitive body, and our physical body, of which collectively are considered to be our temporal being in physical form. There is a fourth dimension and that is our soul aspect. Our authentic self is in agreement with fundamental truths of existence; it is crystal clear and accurate and not limited by our five senses. Our emotions become distorted when we filter our feeling impressions through our conditioned perspectives, thereby interfering with the direct communication stream.

Your emotions serve a very important purpose. They are part of a highly sophisticated alert system. Your physiological response to feeling impressions coupled with your cognitive awareness are the source of your emotions. They can be deceptive in nature because they are not reflection of the highest truths at all times, they are reflections of your interpretations of experience, which is precisely why they are so important. These interpretations often stem from your ego and your conditioning. Your emotions are designed to show you when your thoughts are in synch with actual higher universal truths or when they are in sync with your conditioning (which is, essentially, your past), or the drive to preserve your self-image, or your physical survival, of course.

Negative emotion is a signal that your thinking is out of alignment with the highest actual truth of any given situation. Negative emotions are important because they either expose the maladaptive unconscious beliefs that are driving you or they are like an alert system designed to inform you that it is time to make a change in your life. To change the way you are interpreting a situation, or to change a particular habit that is not serving you, for instance. They show you where you may be holding onto something — an experience, an interpretation, a belief — from your past. Positive emotion signals you to the fact that whatever your thinking, believing, or doing is in alignment with your higher truth. That the path you are heading toward is constructive and adaptive. We often take for granted this simple but profound fact — emotions are nothing more than an innate guidance system. A system that operates with accurate precision. It is up to each of us to learn how to listen to it. The challenge with this is that it requires a particular kind of discretion.

There exists one caveat relevant to the human condition that interferes with our emotional guidance system. It is important to understand the difference between emotions that guide us toward fulfillment and positive growth versus emotions that guide us to further conformity of our default template of reality. The confusion comes from that fact that the later often feels good too. One reason for this is because behaving and thinking in ways from our past produces patterns in our physiology that become very familiar, and the body responds to familiarity with positive emotion. Additionally, any attempts to step outside of what is most familiar causes specific kinds of biological reactions that are uncomfortable.

For instance, if you are familiar with feeling anxious because it has evolved as a learned behavior by seeing it modeled, your cells are used to consistent influxes of cortisol. When you choose to engage in things that cause you to feel relaxation, your cells get a shot of serotonin, but rather than having a positive effect, they begin reacting convulsively because of the discrepancy. It is this discrepancy that causes major discomfort. Then the cognitive distortions come into play and we interpret the feeling as being unfamiliar and, therefore, wrong. To your subconscious mind familiarity is comfortable and safe because it means you are not venturing into unknown territory that may be life threatening — even if what is most familiar is, in actuality, destructive to your overall flourishing.

This example demonstrates how our original exposure to life establishes an invisible box in which we then tend to stay within the parameters of throughout our entire life simply because it is most familiar. This box is reinforced through our biological reactions. The original demonstrated beliefs, projections, and standards we first experienced are integrated as our own in the same way our language is. It are all learned through repetition of exposure until they feel normal. For instance, you may have been born right into a paradigm that "proved" to you that money and struggle are inseparable. In that case, because of your unconscious drive for congruence and comfort in familiarity, your biological responses (which then turn into emotional responses) will lead you to make choices that would serve to again prove this inseparability to be true.

As you can see, the accumulated associations throughout our lifetime are imprinted within our physiology and we become one with that particular reality. This construct then orchestrates our behavior, which creates redundant environmental patterns — together establishing an addictive reciprocity feedback loop. This feedback loop is continually reinforcing our paradigm of reality as an external reality, when in fact, as you can see, it is merely subjective.

So the question is, how do we distinguish between the two — how can we know if the positive emotion is signaling the most effective route to our higher desires and the highest truths of reality, rather than our familiar past? The answer is that we must first expose the falsehoods that we thought defined us. How to do this is presented in upcoming chapters.

# Chapter Five

## Shame: An Epidemic

It's likely that instead of allowing your current emotional gauge to operate purely as your guidance system you have been placing deflectors between it and higher truths thereby interfering with your accurate receptivity of it. As you discover important fundamental truths of you and of existence itself, your conditioned way of seeing the world will begin to crumble. You will generate a new matrix of beliefs constructed out of eternal truths from which to perceive and experience life. After specific conditioned constructs are reconciled the deflectors will no longer exist.

I used to think that the most important question was, how do we ascertain which portions of our conditioning need reorganizing, or complete dismantling, and which portions we should appreciate and exalt more? Now I know that the real question is, how can I love each layer of my conditioned personality and perspective as to give it the attention and honor it deserves — to reintegrate with it without rejecting it — and thus, to heal it from the inside out.

While it is true that if joy defines where we want to go - point B, we must identify point A, so that we can determine how to get there. This requires that we step outside of denial and acknowledge what is actually dominating our reality, but not by then aggressively attempting to destroy the part of ourselves that sees from point A's reality.

A very common conditioned construct (Point A) is represented by a what I call a "Paradigm of Shame". This paradigm is constructed of beliefs which work in unison, whereby they continually feed into each other to sustain the emotion of shame. When we consider that in general true happiness is correlated to how fully our needs are met, specifically our needs for love, certainty, significance, connection, contribution, growth, novelty, meaning and purpose, we gain a sense of where point B is. Ofttimes shame interferes with the fulfillment of these needs.

An additional factor regarding our happiness is relative to the perceived gap between who we are (Point A) and who we think we should be (Point B). Thus, our happiness is relative to the degree that we thinks we fall short of or align with this ideal. That is, if we don't know who we really are. We hereby

Point A is a conglomeration of our conditioned constructs (way of perceiving reality and ourselves relative to it) that prevent our needs from being filled directly and fully, and the ways in which we think we are falling short of our ideals. The purpose of dissecting point A is to expose the un-necessary falsehoods that have attached themselves to you and have prevented you from loving yourself and others to the same degree.To shed light upon point A, I encourage you to consider the question: what does shame believe?

*Shame believes that you are inherently unworthy if you are imperfect.*

We may expect ourselves to embody many ideals at once and find that we are constantly adjusting to fit within them all simultaneously. Often our assumed value depends on double standards that are impossible to fulfill. Trying to live within parameters of perfection are severely detrimental to our happiness, yet it the only way we feel worthy of love. This can lead to a perpetual state of discontent with ourselves — this is shame.

Shame is maintained through a sense of there being something outside yourself, like that of an omnipresent authority figure assessing your behavior, appearance, and thoughts unwaveringly. This presence, seemingly external to you, monitors you based upon the same parameters of goodness that your parents had expected from you or that you had picked up from society. This presence feels as though it is overseeing your level of goodness in every moment, with which peace is often an elusive experience for you. This is likely built upon your initial foundation of experiences with significant authority figures in our childhood. That is, our conceptual idea of an external dictatorship and the ideals expected of us often mirrors the same dynamics (method of authority and expectations) in our early life. Once you make this distinction, you will begin to realize that this superimposed superego has been dictating your feelings of worthiness and well-being even in your adulthood.

Of course, instilling a sense of right and wrong was a critically important part of your development. Although, falling into thoughts of self-condemnation with every mistake you make would be an indication of toxic-shame. With this, you believe that you as a person are wrong or bad, as opposed to your choices being wrong. If your parameters of right and wrong have simply been adopted as your own and never contemplated, they may in fact work against your happiness. Striving to stay within adopted ideals is common because conformity was equivalent to being loved and worthy of belonging. Although in truth, as an adult, shame serves you only if you are upholding your own standards and expectations through them.

A deflated sense of self-worth causes us to focus on our failures, to magnify, and even generate within our imagination scenarios that reinforce our imperfections. Self condemnation has a snowball effect because it causes mistakes themselves to become your focus and thus the direction you continue to move toward. When you believe that your value is reduced with each of these occurrences, you misinterpret the intention of the guidance. To the contrary, efficient response to your mistakes guides you to find resolution or to reassess your direction and choices for the better.

According to the research work of Dr. Maxwell Maltz, surgeon and author of *Psycho-Cybernetics*, our innate guidance is the function of what he coined as our success servo mechanism. He tells us that it operates in exactly the same way that planes do, as a course-correcting function. To reach a desired target, its operation is dependent on its capacity to respond positively (corrective) to negative feedback. As a relative example, with the Apollo mission to the moon, the spacecraft was slightly off course 97 percent of the time; it was on course only 7,500 miles out of 250,000 miles; for the remaining (majority) miles, therefore, it was course correcting. This illustrates the importance of not only being okay with, but welcoming mistakes because most of the time you are just correcting course.

Correct operation of your success mechanism means you are heading toward the accomplishment of an intentional goal...through a series of failures. Focusing on the negative feedback rather than using it to adjust course causes the negative feedback to become the target. By accepting that mistakes are required for your expansion, you also would recognize that the only way to success is through failure. Once you understand that imperfection is the only space that success can be born from, then you can even appreciate it.

In the occurrence of looking back at our "inaccurate" choice we often forget that the choice we made was relative to our awareness at that time. We always make choices that we think will be best according to our values and needs in the moment. Acknowledging the positive intention behind your actions offers self-compassion.

For many of us who have experienced intense emotional discord, we learned to immediately intercept the full manifestation of our negative feelings with cerebral interpretations. These were most often directed inwardly as self-blame. Because our survival was translated through the feeling of being loved and accepted, if this was not unconditionally given we made the assumption that our very worthiness was the determining factor. Here is where we can see the inherent underlying intelligence of shame as to generate a relationship with it — to understand it from a place of compassion. In exalting shame you can realize that it is you having the awareness that you do in fact create your own reality. That everything you experience as "outside" of you has been projected in to your experience of reality by you. That you are fully responsible for your experiences.

Tantric Buddhist philosophy encourages us to recognize the positive intention behind our tendencies and to acknowledge the hidden intelligence from which they were born as a survival strategy. If you are able to see the underlying intelligence of this coping mechanism, you can embrace it and observe it from all angles. This form of observation is part of the Focusing

Method, which I will be guiding you through more of in an upcoming chapter. Ultimately, your tendency to feel shame is not another enemy you must destroy or hate, it is simply a way in which you were coping with reality when you were young. Hating or berating any coping mechanism is like reprimanding a child for not being an adult yet.

Just like with your own imperfections, you do not need to resist the truth that imperfect and uncomfortable conditions or situations will be present in your life. With each interaction with or exposure to the discernment of something unwanted, you gain an awareness of what you prefer. With each of your desires, another actual possibility for you becomes perceivable to you. You can see that all tangible things in physical existence began from a discomfort that identified a desire, that evolved into a deeper contemplation of thought about what was preferred. If allowed to, it then gained momentum in action and became a physical form or experiential interaction.

You, as part of divine intelligence, did not want to experience humanity so that you could escape it. Appreciation for what is, inclusive of challenges, mistakes, failures, and negative emotions, isn't a passive, defeatist kind of acceptance of mediocrity. This one comes on the heels of knowing that you are already complete and perfect within humanity's constructs of incompleteness and infinite becoming.

# *Looking Closer at Self-Deception &*
# *The Great Spiritual Disguise*

Personal experience has shown me that striving to believe in higher truths before genuinely loving ourselves doesn't actually serve our progression. Nor does adhering to spiritual doctrine cause your emotional needs to disappear. We do not benefit from spiritual teachings when they serve to reinforce coping and defense mechanisms originally birthed from not meeting certain emotional needs to begin with.

My original motivations that drove me toward spirituality were simultaneously constructive and destructive. Hidden underneath my desire for comfort, belonging and guidance (which spirituality provides), was also a desire to rise above my humanity. Thus, my spiritual practice itself was a byproduct of shame. It appeared to offer me a way of gaining significance and gave me the false sense that it would eventually bring me to a state of perfection. The desire for and attempt at perfection reflected a plethora of coping strategies I was still holding onto.

Positive change did emerged from this as well. It was through the meditative state of Yoga the I was removed from all underlying anxiety that became so engrained. Most importantly, it caused me to realize that I didn't have to be suffering at all times. It provided the contrast I needed and made me realize that I could step away from that self-hate and anxiety. This is when I started to see beyond my paradigm of suffering, that there were alternative ways of feeling. Although there was a shadow side to this. Our unresolved psychological issues can result in spirituality bypassing. For instance, I was using spiritual practices like meditation, yoga, and the study of spiritual philosophy to justify my antisocial behavior. My isolation was actually motivated by lack of self-esteem, deeply embedded trust issues, and fear of both intimacy and the inevitable conflicts within relationship dynamics.

Avoidance was my way of detaching from my needs and deceiving myself into believing that they did not exist. Avoidance eventually evolved into a fear of commitment and the freedom inherent to non-commitment provided me with a baseline level of safety. In other words, commitment itself was a threat. Moving forward into adulthood, I was extremely cautious of the "danger" inherent to committing to anything because of the inability to escape from it — to avoid it — if need be. my fear-driven escapist habit was actually covering a deep sense of emotional deprivation.

As a result this habit, which had become part of my personality, I was constantly falling short of completing anything that could potentially lock me into a certain way of being in the world. A sense of groundless insecurity evaded me. All the while a contradictory desire for self-actualization and self-realization dominated my conscious thoughts. But neither can never come from self-rejection. The cultivation of our human qualities cannot ensue if we are wanting to escape the human experience all together. As you could imagine with this polarity at play, I found myself never actually living my life fully. I undoubtedly had the actual mental and physical capacity to achieve whatever I wanted, but was simultaneously driven by the fear of commitment and thus, continually sabotaged my efforts.

My unresolved issues eventually transferred to my spiritual practice in another covert way as well. During this time I was particularly drawn to the Buddhist teachings of non-self whereby its philosophies provide insight into how our feelings, perceptions, thoughts, body, and beliefs are impermanent and ultimately out of our constant control and that therefor we do not exist as a permanent self. Yet, there exists within me a strong desire to fulfill my very human and natural need for praise, attention, approval, and connection that I was simultaneously both in denial of and trying to rise above. Because we must meet our needs as part of being human, I found a covert way of meeting them — through the philosophy of not needing them. I thought (unconsciously so) my more spiritual nature would lead to the attention and approval I was really seeking.

Furthermore, at this time I was starting to became highly attuned to what were previously my subconscious reactive patterns — defenses and strong emotional reactions that rose out of context, for instance. This sort of awareness is common when we start to really comprehend the non-self philosophies of Buddhism. This in and of itself can be very good thing — a turning point in our lives, but without the insight of my own true worth and value in tact, recognition of my personality "project" became another venue for which to sink into greater shame. As a result I turned to spirituality, but did not use it as a path toward self-love but rather as a means to get rid of parts of myself that I thought were unworthy and to change myself, thus strengthening the split within me — a split that placed me squarely against myself. While change is always a worthy goal in light of progression if it is inspired by a longing to be more authentic and to live more fully as apposed to crusading against yourself.

Case in point, it is important to acknowledge that spiritual practice can become a bandage that covers your unresolved personal and interpersonal issues. This is precisely why I feel that attending to our psychological well-being should supra cede spiritual practice of any sort. Ignoring human psychology does not serve to uplift humanity in any honorable way — we have all seen the atrocity that can occur in the name of religion and spirituality. Unhealed aspects of our being and personality always find expression in either covert or overt ways, this is simply inevitable. Both spirituality and religion can becomes a sort of venue through which people live out their unresolved past in destructive ways.

Our coping mechanisms designed to block our vulnerability and reject our needs, and our shame can become intertwined and come forth in many different disguises, not just in the form of spiritual bypassing per se. To further exemplify this, consider again how, as a child of an alcoholic parent, some common unmet needs were that of positive mirroring, adequate attention, security, and proper guidance.

One of my covert ways of feeling seen, validated, and loved was wrapped up in being good and in saving my mother. I was always the one that made her feel better, who boosted her self-esteem by conforming to her definition of a good girl. I began to see that I couldn't actually save her as I got older. I saw my mother's depression and helplessness and felt terrible guilt for not removing her from this pain, so of course I ventured into the world of healing. At the time I did not recognize the true motive behind this choice. I can see now that I was unconsciously assuming that the more wisdom I gained, the more likely I can then provide that for her and heal her broken heart. Also, it is no wonder that I decided to write a book about emotional healing, of which in turn, the cycle of shame continued.

My efforts in writing the first version of this book were still being motivated by unconscious desires and attempts at fulfilling emotional needs that hadn't been met. Additionally, my shame transferred over to this effort as well. I placed a virtual magnifying glass over every single potential imperfection with every word I wrote. I was interested in writing because I could alter everything to the point that it was perfect — and this way no-one would have to know that it started out imperfect. It was my "perfect" guise. I'd be showing the world that I was intelligent, that I had depth, that I could save them, that I was spiritual (good), and I could present it all when it is finally perfect without them seeing the struggle of making it so. As you can see, the original version of this book reflected one big coping mechanism.

Fortunately, now that I have experienced an incredible journey of emotional alchemy through a process of learning to genuinely love myself I can engage in my spiritual practices more authentically. With this, their positive impact upon my life has set coarse and I bring this version of this book to you with a genuine desire to provide you with guidance toward appreciation, inner-contentment, and self-love.

Essentially, the constructive use of self-awareness starts with the gradual recognition of our most prevalent self-deceptions. Our deception hides behind certain kinds of motives that drive our habitual, and often destructive choices. By mindfully investigating the motives behind our actions we can expose our emotional wounds and the beliefs that rule us. The emotion behind our motives is always either fear — a perceived threat to our survival or to our self image in some way or another — or desire. With proper investigation we can come to understand how our motives formed and why they continue to dominate us.

Each of us has experienced three stages of increased autonomy — toddler, adolescent, and adulthood — that mark significant transitions from emotional and psychological entanglement with our caregivers (usually parents and sometimes our siblings) to incremental degrees of autonomous separation. Within these stages we develop an understanding of boundaries and ambitions of the self. Individuation marks the development of a sense of self. When there are unresolved negative emotional experiences within the context of our individuation particularly, they often become the heartbeat of our most hidden ulterior motives — especially the motive of fear of not belonging, not being loved or valued.

One common function of ulterior motives is the seeking of external validation and significance in an effort to feel a greater sense of worth as in my personal examples above. The problem with all ulterior motives is that life will always "prove" to you more of what you believe to be true. That is, if your true motive is to feel worthy, you therefore must hold the belief that you are not. In which case, you will continue to create circumstances that "prove" to yourself that you are not yet worthy. Our hidden motives both cause us to unconsciously recreate our internal issues externally again and again — just in different contexts — in an attempting to resolve them internally.

Your experience of life continually reflects all of your energetic frequencies stored within the three dimensions of your being — most significantly is your emotional being. While our feeling impressions are intangible, they always show up in the expression of physical evidence as our conditions and circumstances. Emotion is the dominant driver; the most influential over your actions and attractions. Thus, each shift in your emotion, your state of being, inherently initiates a different point of consciousness and of attraction — a parallel reality to be experienced by you.

Any compensation or striving to prove something is an indication that you are still within whatever that frequency range of consciousness and belief is. Thus, your actions are motivated by your attempt to prove it wrong. This only inadvertently strengthens the original belief because the motivation itself reinforces it to be true. This is the workings of the ego, and there is no other way around it than to realize that it can only be true — that you are unworthy. That is, from that particular level of consciousness.

Just as the universe is infinite, so too are our levels of consciousness. Each of these levels hold their own truths. The way to transcend them is not by fighting the beliefs embedded within them, rather by surrendering to them. You must first surrender to them because we can only see from the perspective, the point of view, wherein the belief resides. Therefore, when you surrender to a belief you remove yourself form its self-perpetuating loop. In doing so, you will begin to clearly see the true motive behind your actions.

Getting to the truth of the motives behind your actions or inactions will help you recognize your wounds so that you can attend to them effectively. In doing so, eventually your motives will not stem from attempts to fulfill your unmet needs rather, from a pure inspiration, and this is when things begin to fall into place for you.

To remain unaware of the motives behind our habits is very seductive because it requires no courage to directly face our unresolved past and our fears. Ultimately, the alternative to conscious self-awareness is suppression of your human potential and rejection of positive possibility. The results of unawareness are lost opportunities to love, authentically serve with your gifts, and experience the fullness of life itself.

# Chapter Six
## The Language of Unresolved Memories

It is often difficult to recognize the emotions and beliefs driving us. This is because we have created coping mechanisms, which are maintained by self-deception and keep us oblivious to our underlying emotions and beliefs. There are two common types of self-deception, at times, simultaneously active in contradictor ways. On one hand, we are not cognizant of how we are being in the world relative to how we think we are. This is marked by ego defense mechanisms, of which denial and projection are most commonly understood. These defenses are temporarily constructive in that they superficially preserve our self-esteem in very specific situations and interactions, although ultimately, what they actually produce are more difficulties in our life. They block us from seeing past them into the heart of what is truly at their core.

Self-preservation filters cause us to think that we are correct and justified in our actions, when in fact we may not be. We may in fact be reacting from a past unresolved wound in a way that is overly aggressive, or dismissive, or suspicious, just to name a few resulting actions. We create delusional stories that support our position and assume that our thoughts and our reactions to these thoughts are justified and rational. What we are actually doing is reacting to old triggers thereby, unconsciously bringing unresolved emotional wounds from the past into our present and creating stories from them in real time. Most often our perceptions are completely screwed and misplaced our of alignment with reality.

While it is more common to avoid acknowledging the non-admirable aspects of ourselves — our child-like reactions stemming from our the past, which we've woven into our perception of the present — to keep our egos intact, oftentimes we simultaneously do the opposite. We cultivate negative self-destructive perceptions about ourselves that are untrue; these being the engine that sustains feelings of shame. These types of thoughts that reiterate things that seem rational, but in fact are not grounded in reality are coined cognitive distortions. For instance, after social interactions, you may reflect over your behavior in a very unfavorable light. You draw upon the the most damaging explanation rather than the most logical one. You take the negative details and magnify them while filtering out all positive aspects of a situation. Personalization is one type of cognitive distortion; we all know someone who seems to believe that almost everything others do or say is some kind of direct, personal reaction to, or attack against, them. This is because they are carrying around emotional experiences that have left them extremely sensitive to judgment and criticism.

Throughout the book when using the term

"trauma", despite its dramatic connotation, I am referring to any experience that has negatively impacted you which, for any number of reasons, you have not yet resolved. This could seem relatively minor or quite considerable. The only importance is the degree to which it affected, and continues to affect you. Sometimes a seemingly minor occurrence can cause a significant impact, and sometimes a seemingly significant occurrence can have little to no impact upon you both consciously or unconsciously.

When we are confronted with associations to our unresolved pain (triggers), our reactions often exemplify childish behavior motivated by strong defensive positioning. This is because in whatever manner we had originally reacted to the original trauma, this continues to be our same response as an adult. Our defensive positioning and attachment to our perception and to justifying our behavior and emotional response remains because our minds are deceiving us into believing that we are correct in our perception. We often don't even realize that we are acting like a child. And we often remain completely oblivious to the actual reality of the situation and to the perception of the other people or person involved. For instance, if we had reacted aggressively to our confusion and emotional pain in the past, the same response will be activated from us when associations occur. Then our perception of the situation will conform to support an aggressive "response".

We stay the same emotional age well over many years if we do not transcend those reactions through establishing resolution. Awareness and effective utilization of these trigger occurrences is the most efficient means to uncovering the aspects of yourself that need validation, adequate attention, compassion, resolve, and understanding.

Self-compassion is knowing that each of our intense negative visceral reactions is a stored emotion resurfacing and is the reinforcement of a belief that stemmed from the stored emotional signature. Your inner child (or adolescent, or young adult) is showing you precisely where you have not healed your past.

The very first step to your freedom and growth beyond your past is to observe all components of your intense negative visceral reactions. That is, to observe your thoughts in real time (metacognition), or the emotional signatures, or your behavior in response to the occurrence. After this awareness settles in you will be ready for the feeling signature integration process I described in the previous chapter. I realize that observing yourself this directly may seem foreboding or intimidating, but once you begin to see the positive results of this process in your life you will realize that sinking into the darkness is the only means to your liberation from it. When you can see yourself in these contexts you are no longer immersed in them and you can see them for what they are. Being aware of this means you are perceiving your reactions objectively.

Additionally, you are validating them as being present while you are simultaneously experiencing them as separate from you. Intentionally detaching yourself from them is not a destructive form of escapism. When you observe your thoughts, feelings and actions, you are one step removed from them and thus, they are no longer controlling you. Your creative, higher self is in control.

# Shadow Work:
## Shedding Light Upon Our Judgments

Some well-established and highly effective tools for integration include the Focusing Method, Shadow Work and Inner-Child Work. Shadow work is about exposing the aspects of your personality and the desires and fears you have rejected so that you can address them or use them for your benefit, as we've covered in depth in previous chapter (regarding our judgments, over-compensation, and self deception). Inner-child work is about healing the past so that you can stop living in the past , whether you are doing so consciously or not. These modalities embrace the fact that even though your memories are self-generated points of perceptual awareness, it is important to tap into what was true for you at the time, which may or may not have been the objective truth or the truth from the perspective of those involved. These two modalities coupled with mindful investigation in our feeling signatures and felt experiences are most transformative.

As defined, in Jungian (re. Carl Jung, a Swiss psychiatrist and psychoanalyst who founded analytical psychology) the shadow or "shadow aspect" refers to an unconscious aspect of the personality in which the conscious ego does not identify in itself. Our shadow is the source of both our non-constructive habitual patterns and our greatest dormant qualities. Because we tend to reject or remain ignorant of the least desirable aspects of our personality, the shadow is largely negative. There are, however, positive aspects that may also remain hidden in one's shadow (especially in people with low self-esteem). The shadow includes everything outside the light of consciousness, and may be positive or negative. The densest elements of your shadow aspects have formulated much of your paradigm — your typical way of feeling and perceiving and your most common conditions and dynamics of grace or struggle in each aspect of your life.

You may already know that both your fascination and indignation of people are reflections of yourself to one degree or another. You have the traits of every person you think highly of, and every person you think less of. In knowing this, your judgments can offer up a treasure chest of self-awareness — into the aspects of your personality that you are suppressing. This is very powerful because an important avenue to the deliberate creation of our lives is through the expression of our authentic self.

Our shadow aspects are part of our authentic selves and until they are exposed and accepted, they rule our choices and maintain our deepest inner conflicts. Let's say for instance, that you had an overtly aggressive and excessively pessimistic parent. As you gained more autonomous awareness, not only did you begin to dislike this trait, you felt embarrassed by it. You began to detest it the parent and as they continued to express themselves this way, you further deepened your hatred toward those behaviors — and the rejection and denial of these same feelings within yourself. This then can lead to an imbalance and can perpetuate a split within whereby you continue to deny, reject, suppress, and disown parts of yourself. When you do this, you send these aspects of you, these truths of you, to your subconscious. The subconscious always finds expression because it is an integral part of you. Except sometimes, when it finds expression under your radar of awareness, it does so in harmful ways; ways that are counterproductive to your actual desires.

Returning to the example above, because you had decided to never acknowledge negativity and to never express your anger, you continue to deny that there is abuse and atrocity in the world, and thus never contribute to its healing. Yet, you have a conscious desire to contribute in a profound way. Hence, an internal conflict ensues. Or perhaps, you have denied your own assertiveness, and thus, you have very little boundaries and this often leaves you feeling walked all over by others. There are many other ways our shadows can play themselves out in our lives.

The highest truth is the we can only see our own interpretation of others. This is not them; it is a reflection of them filtered through our perceptions. The people we judge are only reflections of ourselves. Knowing this can assist you in becoming fully self-aware, and integrating this awareness can assist you in becoming whole. You can choose to use the specific traits you admire and those you detest in ways that can benefit you tremendously.

The blessings of this kind of self-awareness can be profound. If you allow and exalt the rejected aspects of yourself, and intelligently apply them to applicable situations in your life, they will significantly contribute to its flourishing. The more whole and authentic you are, the more conscious your choices are and the more empowered you become. The more you accept others for who they are by recognizing that they are aspects of you, the deeper your connections will be. Not only this, but also by recognizing that ultimately their personalities were, like your own, constructed as a byproduct of highly intelligent coping mechanisms originally driven by the need and desire to be loved and accepted by others, the closer your connections will be. This is important because the quality of our connections is universally the highest contributing factor influencing our level of happiness.

# Relationships: Our Greatest Catalysts

There is no question that our unresolved emotional wounds always reflect in our relationship dynamics. Suppression of certain relational fears rooted in survival indirectly sabotage our relationships or prevent positive ones from ever developing in the first place. Our relationships can expose us to our deepest fears and can offer up a treasure chest of self-awareness into aspects of our past that needs compassionate attention and effective resolution. Our fears can significantly interfere with or completely prevent quality connections from evolving. Our particular sensitivities are based upon fear of rejection, abandonment, or entrapment, depending on the nature of our previous hurt.

If in your young life you perceived love continually being withdrawn from you every time your parent went to work for instance, you consequently may fear abandonment. You may be in a relationship, but simultaneously resist true connection and intimacy. Only a very limited degree of vulnerability is permitted; knowing that the exposure of our inner world is within a range of our ability to control. On the other hand, if you had experienced a high degree of enmeshment, you were strongly discouraged from developing your own feelings and preferences. In this case it is highly likely that a fear of commitment dominates your relationships. In which case, you may become triggered by your partners attempts at securing a greater commitment from you.

To know truths about ourselves often requires some discomfort at first, which makes it incredibly easy to succumb to our subconscious ability to deny and distort our (over)reactions as reasonable and justified. "Rather than using the discomfort as motivation to change, we project, deny and justify our reactions to the pain — not knowing that the original pain is what we are reacting to, not the current situation that mirrors it somehow. Because of the discomfort in allowing our emotions and actions to be fully examined, we manipulate reality and interpretations of our behaviors." — Dr. Cortney S. Warren, Professor of Psychology and Professor of Psychiatry, and Author of *Lies We Tell Ourselves, The Psychology of Self Deception*. To shift away from this kind of self-deception I highly suggest that you observe your intense visceral reactions and your judgments wisely. To use them as opportunities to see both what needs healing and which characteristics could contribute to your happiness, should you choose to allow them to emerge in a constructive ways. Doing this consistently can significantly improve your life.

As you become more self-aware, the unfitting beliefs relevant to your past will either simply dissolve or continue to abruptly present themselves to you. The ones that are useless to your newly transformed self, yet remain within this transition and become exposed, are offering opportunities to heal further. This is why I highly suggest as a self-care regimen a relatively regular practice of integration.

In utilizing your strong emotional reactions to move you swiftly along your transformation I invite you to look more deeply into your relationships. Our romantic relationships especially tend to offer up an abundance of triggers because it was within the context of relationships and love that our greatest emotional hurt was experienced. We can become cognizant of our reactions to others as they fall within the framework of cognitive distortions and ego defense mechanisms, initiating deeper reflections into why we are responding these particular ways.

Through analysis of the personalities of the most significant people in our lives, we are outwardly exposed to our shadow aspects. This hints at our emotional past because we rejected certain traits upon learning that they were wrong in some way. Our original reasons for suppressing aspects of our authentic self were because we formulated a belief that these aspects caused more harm than good, or that they make us a bad, unlovable person in some way. It was most important to be lovable and accepted by our family because our survival was dependent upon this. Nevertheless, because wholeness is our natural state we are often feel drawn to people who overtly express the deeply repressed aspects of our own personality. Creating relationships with them is driven by a highly unconscious attempt at re-integration. The more unresolved trauma we have experienced, the more this is the case. Essentially, the purpose behind our relationship unions are our unconscious attempt at wholeness existentially.

We also inhibit aspects of our personality that are constructive and healthy. For example, many of us have suppressed our confidence because we had concluded that confidence and arrogance are one and the same. In which case, we decided to reject it in ourselves. Now we struggle with feelings of worthlessness and expressing our strengths to the world for fear of being labeled as arrogant. Yet, we are nevertheless smitten by people who are confident and wish to be like them.

Attention to negative traits feels like repulsion and attention to positive traits feels like admiration, either way is a reflection into ourselves. When we vehemently reject certain characteristics such as apathy, possessiveness, and impulsiveness, we tend to exhibit their opposite to an imbalanced and unhealthy extreme as an over-compensation. On this same note, someone who is repulsed by the attitude of entitlement may rarely allow themselves to receive, or may never assert themselves in asking for what they want. As a consequence of this they feel as if their life is not as joyful and prosperous as it could be.

In the case of people who are perturbed by laziness, for instance, they likely feel the constant impulse to be productive, but to the detriment of their health and well-being. They fall into the trap of over-compensation — to continue to "prove" that they are not lazy. If you can recognize that the denial and rejection of that particular trait is not serving you, you can allow it back into your personality to a healthy and constructive degree. This may surprise you, but even rejected destructive (inherently negative) traits can be transmuted, exalted, and applied productively in your live.

In balancing out our over-compensations it is important that we heal the unresolved occurrence related to our original decision to suppress these aspects of ourselves. It is also very helpful to also identify the benefits associated with keeping them that way. For instance, someone may be irresponsible (suppressing their responsible nature) in specific areas because it puts them in situations where they have to be rescued time and again; and being rescued causes them to feel cared for and loved. With this their need for love is being fulfilled indirectly and through ulterior motives driving their behavior. This is why it is of incredible importance to learn how to attend to our needs directly.

# Chapter Seven
## Emotional Alchemy: The Remedy for Self-Deception

While it is true that, in accordance with the actual mechanics of the universe your past has absolutely no relationship to your present, just acknowledging this is not enough to change anything. Altering all of your previously configured and habitually sustained biochemical activities which have been influencing your moment to moment choices is not realistic until proper attention to your past is given. Your habitual patterns have been responding to your subconscious beliefs for many years. It is therefore most effective and efficient to resolve your past rather than to try to convince yourself that your past has no impact on your present reality.

Your emotional wounds should not be overlooked in pseudo efforts in personal transformation. Altering the deeply rooted behaviors that lead to unwanted conditions before addressing the causation of them will ultimately lead us to greater struggle and can actually reinforce the very thing we wish to change. To ignore the reason for why you are continually re-creating patterns that do not serve your happiness would be like taking medication to disguise a disease without addressing or attending to the source. Sometimes too, the imagination reinforces the disease. Nevertheless, the disease, or imagination of it, would continue to grow until what masked it is no longer effective.

For this reason, this chapter shows you how to effectively address unintegrated, unresolved negative memories that you may already be conscious of, and those which you have suppressed. This is the next descent into yourself.

My personal experience is evidence that the integration of Inner Child Work and Shadow Work through the Focusing Method can be a very powerful way to rewire the neural-networks and hormonal communication streams that are sustaining the emotional addictions they had established. Emotional addictions are therefore addressed according to your current issues or feelings about yourself and your life; they are not arbitrary pulled up from your past. Keep in mind that if your previous negatively charged experiences have not generated self-defeating beliefs and emotional habits, a historical dig of this sort would be unnecessary and it could generate perceived problems that are not actually affecting you.

As I mentioned in the beginning of this book, my encouragement to intentionally reflect upon your emotional pain is not an invitation for self-pity. Rather, it is an invitation for your awakening, from which clarity and true empowerment will prevail. This is when you become clear about your heart's desires and not only your capacity to create, but also your own deserving to receive. As you heal your emotional body and remember your inherent resources, what has been wanting to be realized through you will begin to do so efficiently. Necessary actions will be guided by intuitive, clear and highly effective impulses, for the most part. This is really about realizing that the universe intends for something specific to be expressed through you. Acting on your inspiration ignites the state of *flow*. This state of being increases your productivity tenfold and applying your efforts toward the advancement of humanity then evokes within you a greater sense of purpose.

# Uncovering The Deepest Layers

Each time the belief is reinforced through our thoughts, emotions, and their resulting environment they become more and more automatic, descending more deeply below our level of awareness. They eventually become so subtle and so automatic we have no idea that they are controlling our perceptions and choices.

One contributing factor for the retention of emotional signatures, which lead to many of our beliefs, is related to the function of the autonomic nervous system. Until we develop the anatomical structures in adulthood that allow us the ability to mindfully respond to perceived threats, our body's autonomic nervous system controls our reactions to them completely. Our sympathetic nervous system can respond to adversity, which include emotionally traumatic experiences, in only three ways — fight, flight, or freeze. These reactions create an unintentional psycho/emotional/biological "split" and detachment from your true self and generate an emotional elixir that becomes habitual if the original cause is not properly addressed. If we freeze, we send the experience to the subconscious in order to return to a physiological state of balance. If we physically escape, we never find psycho-emotional resolution and thus, repress the experience. If we fight, we find ourselves under even greater threat. The greater the threat, the more likely we have to repress it in order to cope and bring your body back to a state of homeostasis.

With any of these three reactions, we send the experience and it's accompanied emotions into the deepest recesses of our subconscious mind. This is why it is through both the emotional body and cognitive perceptions that the malleability of our neurochemistry exists. More on this coming up.

Dr. Dispenza uses his scientific research to explain the effects of unresolved emotional experiences. "Every time we have an intense emotional reaction, a chemical elixir is created and the emotions linger for days [if not properly resolved]. This creates 'a mood.' If it remains for weeks to months, it forms our temperament and if unaddressed for years, it evolves into a personality trait. Considering this chemical elixir created in the body is highly addictive, we become unconsciously addicted to the emotion to reaffirm who we are. In this case, you may consciously want to change, but you have memorized an emotion that has become part of your identity and your conditional tendencies accordingly." We are, in effect, hypnotized by them at this point.

Aside from remembering everything we have ever learned, as well as the data existing within the collective unconscious, our subconscious mind remembers everything we ever experienced with our senses and with our feelings. The "split" I spoke of above is between what is conscious to you and what you have suppressed, repressed, denied or rejected in respect to your feeling based experiences and their effect on your personality and choices.

This is why sometimes simply your awareness of a shadow aspect of yourself alone can cause a significant shift. Although, this doesn't automatically equate to an emotional resolution relative to the original causation of the fragmentation. Integration is the re-emergence with yourself through both awareness and resolution of the original experiences. This is why integrative healing modalities offer the most effective techniques for mending psycho/emotional fractures.

I will show you how to use your feeling signatures and felt-experiences as guides that lead you back to the experiences that have both cultivated and continue to perpetuate inner conflict and how to effectively address them. The way of accessing suppressed emotion is through your felt-experiences. Those that stem from your past can be brought forth into your current time space reality and felt with constructively. Because your feeling body is familiar with the direct source of the trauma you can revisit the original experience intuitively, led by your feeling impressions, and address the very initial emotional causation of your current belief structures. By altering the embedded memory of the experience you are altering the internal effect it had within you.

The first step, though, is to increase your awareness of the responses within the body as you interact with others and the world in general. I encourage you to consciously observe your feeling signatures and felt-experiences on a daily basis.

That is, to completely meet and open to the raw immediacy of experience. As a wise spiritual teacher once said, "If we actually feel the living quality, the texture of the emotions as they are in their naked state, then the experience also contains ultimate truth. We discover that the emotion actually does not exist as it appears, but it contains much wisdom." Feeling signatures contain a certain essence that can be articulated, and with meditative inquiry linked to a past causal experience.

The Focus Method is a means to accessing your past through meditative inquiry and hyper awareness of felt-sensations. "The Focus Method offers an unfolding experience whereby you allow your felt experience to guide your exploration into an issue. It is a process of unfoldment and discovery beginning with an expanded awareness of the felt experience, to a conscious sinking into it, and then in articulating it from various angles until the causation is revealed", writes author of *Towards a Psychology of Awakening,* John Welwood. The felt experience will shift and in turn you will gain a new perspective and valuable insight into what you had been believing which led you right to the problem. With this wisdom within your awareness you can address it accordingly.

When the feeling signature shifts by virtue of you being present with it, you bring your current level of awareness into the past experience thereby transmuting the original feeling signature. By bringing light to and resolving each piece — each significantly impactful experience which you have rejected or suppressed — you will cause your current paradigm to reconstruct from the inside out.

This process of integration calls for bringing yourself to a state of complete calm whereby your brainwave patterns enter into a Alpha-Theta brainwave frequency. This state will allow you to access memories and stored emotion effectively because it removes you from the restraints of time and space, your external conditions and habitual thought patterns. This offers the purest communication with your emotional body and allows you to tap into your authentic self. The deeply calm brainwave state allows you to create a new story about yourself.

This is a gradual process of unfolding — of discovery and emotional alterations. We can deliberately alter our subconscious only to the extent to which we alter the "things" it is composed of — beliefs and emotional signatures (memories) — in the fashion in which they were created. That is with either repetition during a particular brainwave state that allows access to communication with the subconscious mind, or in singular high intensity states.

Although, it's worth noting that despite the subtle, deliberate, and  graceful nature of meditative states, they actually lead to relatively efficient and, certainly, powerful integration. Meditation coupled with mindful reflection offers a refined receptivity.

With mindful investigation, you carefully descend into the layers of your cellular memories from which important realizations emerge to your consciousness. With these practices you will begin to pick up momentum and the rate at which things become clearer and more obvious will expedite.

The Focusing Method will likely lead you to the realization that some form of inner-child work is necessary for resolution to your epiphanies as they unfold. When you are immersed into the emotion consciously it oscillates between sinking into its felt experience and your cognitive reflection of its messages. The messages come to you naturally, you do not seek them. From here you can attend to the inception of the emotional pattern with love and validation. This is because to resolve your past is to allow the emotional signature to transform into equilibrium through positive closure. This is done by meeting the needs that weren't met at the time, which were to feel validated, loved, accepted, and secure. These needs cannot be denied, they were the most important necessities to your very survival. Their lack thereof is the only reason for the experience of trauma to any extent.

To illustrate what I mean by revisiting and properly attending to the needs of your inner-child, as an option you can envision the exalted or higher-self version of the other person involved and have them attend to you the way you needed at the time. Alternatively, you can imagine responding to them the way you wish you could have at the time had your life not depended on them. Perhaps instead you could imagine the presence of another person whom you trust as they provide you with what you needed at that time. It is only important to feel into your visualization and create a scenario that truly feels nurturing and protective. No matter how you find relief, it is important to continue to be with the resolution until it is felt as if it did happen this way. This brings into the original experience a sense of having control within the occurrence itself. It does not justify it or approve what happened or how you were treated; it simply removes its negative control over you and resolves the split within. In the absolute sense, nothing in our life has meaning other than what we attach to it.

With mindful investigation and self-compassion there is no need to keep your truth or your past suppressed or hidden. With this type of practice you will be restructuring the memory by soothing yourself back to emotional stability, in effect resolving the trauma within your feeling body. After which, you may find yourself ready to deliberately shift your perception of the experience to a more constructive interpretation. I am suggesting that you may be ready for an objective perspective, not saturated with suppression, denial, or dissociation of your emotions — a perspective stemming from a higher place of truth.

Ultimately, soothing yourself by giving to yourself what you needed at the time of the original occurrence alters the causation of the experience and your biological attachment to it. With this many of the symptomatic (biochemical) associations eventually cease to exist and as a result, the consequential surface conditions will shift. This is because the absence of the physiological addiction to the unresolved emotion allows for new core beliefs to take shape. Reality always conforms to your beliefs, so as your point of awareness shifts, your projection of reality will shift.

Additionally, it is important to know that with repetition and emotional weight, thoughts change our neural networks. They are eventually integrated into our being and personality. Scientific research supporting neuroplasticity shows us that we have the ability to change the actual structure and activity of our brains to reflect our thoughts. That is, our brain structures change to accommodate our newly imagined realities. To paraphrase Dr. Dispenza, we can make our thoughts so real that our brain actually changes to seem as though the event has already become our physical reality.

With this work, the realizations that come forth evolve in an expansive multi-layered fashion whereby every layer of realization leads to greater understanding and expansion. The deeper you delve into your subconscious, the more profound your realizations, and thus, the more profound your integration. Although each realization pulls from deeper aspects of your subconscious, it results in broader and higher perspectives, like how the layers of an onion become larger as they extend out from the center.

Each shift in your paradigm, whether subtle of profound, is necessary for full healing and integration to take place. With this evolution, you may experience the same external condition or challenge again and again. It is important to keep in mind that you are getting closer and closer to resolution with every consecutive reoccurrence. Although, from your perspective you see the pattern re-emerge not realizing that it is being experienced from a higher level of consciousness. You are never going back, you are always progressing even if it appears otherwise.

As another precaution, when you begin exploring this method you will experience what could be considered "high-level" confusion. You will see yourself reacting and you will still react just as you have been for years, or decades even. With this, the body is still in the past, but your intellect is not and you will likely experience an intensified sense of cognitive dissonance as a result. I assure you that it is part of the process and I urge you to stay with it as it evolves. This is you becoming self-aware on a deeper level. This is you increasing to a new level of consciousness, one that is in greater alignment with the actual truth of realty vs. one constructed from your past. This is a much better place to be in than low-level confusion whereby you are fully consumed by the chaos of survivalist biological reactions (even when it is completely unnecessary) without even knowing it. When this is the case, you think the illusion is real. You are thrown around by old reactions to old associations without direction, intention, or clarity.

Soon enough you will experience your new perception far removed from the old emotional/ biological addictions as normal and you will then realize how far you have come. As you are going through it remind yourself that all this means is that you are on your way to transcending the old and at the beginning stage of entering a state of pure intentional creation whereby you will come in union with clarity and intention.

Essentially, all aspects of your shadow have something to say. When you actually listen they will feel the validation they had been wanting all along. Otherwise you will continue to keep them contained within your subconscious and by virtue of their camouflage, they will continue to influence your life negatively. These are inclusive to who you are; you cannot "unown" them by rejecting them. You can love them, and then listen to them. They always have a message. Their messages always carry the resolution to them. Once resolved through the process of meeting the need that was missing at the time they will transmute on their own. With this, you have not continued to feed your rejection of them, instead you have listened to them and then instead of staying frozen, they are free to evolve. Feelings, in their healthy state, always evolve; this is their natural rhythm.

Truths about ourselves that we refuse to accept and attend to in a healthy resolve, is a covert attempt at dis-ownership of them. This results in psychological and emotional fragmentation. Fragmentation is innately destructive, while wholeness is innately constructive and adaptive. The strength inherent to unity offers evidence that wholeness is our most empowered and natural state. It is therefore the fragmentation of ourself that contributes most to our sense of disempowerment. Wholeness is the same as self love, and inherent to self love is love and appreciation for others. The more you love yourself, the easier it will be to constructively address these deeper complexities of your relationships with both your intimate connections and the world at large.

I invite you to think of you and your life symbolically represented as a home. Perhaps for the most part, the windows drapery are closed as a result of emotional habits and self-rejection. Nevertheless, the light is still present, it is just being blocked from permeating through the windows. Upon each new experience of reclamation, light naturally enters. Sometimes this is a gradual and subtle, like the morning sun rise. Other times it is instantaneous and profound, like the sunlight piercing through a sudden unexpected opening in the blanket of dense clouds.

Once your shadow aspects are seen, exalted, and integrated you will re-establish wholeness and alignment. With this, your previously untapped qualities will become active. The more resources you have to pull from within yourself, the more equipped you are with productively handling life's challenges. This is when challenges themselves can be seen, understood, and known as blessings in disguise. Your life will become warmer and brighter as a result. Storms will still come, but those that normally would leave residue on your windows, blurring your vision of positive possibility, will no longer do so. The light will permeate because of the relative absence of any unnecessary and excessively enduring obstructions. You will see that any "obstacles" are ultimately there to face you toward the best direction, down the correct hallway and up the right flight of stairs. They are simply present in your experience to serve your progression.

Your realization, in and of itself, that the darkness of your pain can be transformed into the most vibrant light of love and compassion, establishes a starting point for the creation of a new paradigm; one that is more congruent with your truth and hospitable to the cultivation of your desires. You will begin to experience greater serendipity and engagement with others that help you with the unfolding of your ambitions. From here, deliberate focus upon what you are wanting to create will be much more effective and your potential will give way to desired results, rather than more of what you keep trying to keep away.

# Resistance to Integration

Integration calls for stepping into your pain, and this, in turn, requires courage like no other. It is quite common to feel resistance to releasing your pain knowing that in order to do so you must re-merge with it once again. The good news is that if you go through with the integration/healing process until it is complete, this will be the very last time you will need to visit that specific pain. This, in contrast to re-living it in covert ways over and over again throughout the rest of you life. Hopefully you can see that integrating aspects of yourself that you have suppressed and rejected is well worth the effort and time because it will pay off for the rest of your life.

There are three generalized categories of people relative to their openness to integration. The first are those who are oblivious to the impact their past is having on their current life. These people have suppress and repressed their past to very high degree. These people, like most, do not want to continue living a victimized experience of life at all, they just aren't aware of that they are reacting to the past and that they have the option to integrate. On the other hand, some people hold tightly onto their difficult past for the purpose of maintaining a justification for their adulthood struggles, without the desire or intent to resolve the original source of their emotional issues. Lastly, some people resists resolution to their emotional pain because they are holding onto it as a means to fulfill needs such as significance, certainty, or connection. The process offered in this book for attending to the causation of your emotional pain is not for the purpose of attaching yourself to a perspective that you are a victim; it is in fact the exact opposite. It will release you from the belief that you must be in pain to receive the love you need.

To generalize here, the first category are perhaps even unaware of the extent to which their past has led to their current struggle with things like diminished self-esteem and confidence. Paradoxically, while their motive behind their denial is in light of self-preservation simply because the experiences were too painful, they do not know who they really are. Their stages of individuation did not provide them with adequate or accurate mirroring of themselves. We learn, or discover, who we really are when others accurately mirror back to us who we are. If they do not accurately reflect back to us who we are due to their own neurosis or elusiveness, our idea of who we are is distorted and inaccurate.

While the second — those who hold tightly onto their story without the intent to completely resolve their emotional anchors — have a very different motive — they fear that they are incapable of providing it for themselves. This too is in light of self-preservation.

As for the third category, in response to their current life struggle they receive sympathy and attention that satisfies their need for love, significance, and belonging. Others may see these people as "drama queens", whereby there is always a catastrophe taking place in their life, and the people of the first generalized category as walking around pretending to be someone they are not. This is because they do not know who they really are. Either way, they both feel unworthy of being loved — without the drama and without the mask. To reiterate, these examples are generalizations.

Part of this type of self-directed healing work leads to identifying unacknowledged benefits that serve to keep us stuck. If after you give yourself the validation you seek and attend to your emotional wounds with greater compassion and understanding, you continue to choose to hold onto them, the very next step is to seek out their potential hidden benefits. Which is to say, to acknowledge how you are getting certain needs met by holding onto your emotional pain. From here you can then choose whether it is worth having them met indirectly this way, or to meet them directly in ways that are constructive.

Often we develop beliefs that support of our resistance such as: releasing my suffering is equivalent to me condoning the poor treatment I received from others. If this is the case, forgiveness is the only remedy. While forgiveness cannot be forced, it can be encouraged through shifting your perspective. It is easier to forgive others if you can see how the difficulties they caused you have contributed to your life in beneficial and meaningful ways. That is, how these specific experiences have contributed to the fulfillment of your destiny. Perhaps you can see how they helped you formulate your highest values and convictions. This approach does not require you to continue thinking of the experience as one that is justified or approved of. Rather, it shifts to a means-to-an-end that serves you rather than stops you.

It is also important to forgive yourself. If you ask yourself how you have been reinforcing that original experiences and the beliefs stemming from it, and how have they played out in your life for all these years, the answers will come. From here you can forgive yourself for seeing things from that point of limited awareness. You must understand that you developed these patterns from a place of goodness — they were birthed by you as defenses to protect your heart or to maintain a sense of connection. Then you may realize that you are ready to let go of the physical manifestations they had caused and ask the universe what is the next step for you, the answer will come.

In general, you will become a positive influence within all seven spheres of your life — spiritual, intellectual, physical, financial, familial, vocational, and social, because your beliefs surrounding and supporting the dynamics within them will shift. You will be the generator of peace and happiness within your relationships, rather than taking the stance that others should act a certain way toward you at all times in order for you to be happy. While your emotional needs — growth, certainty, novelty, contribution, significance, and connection — will remain, the fulfillment of them will exist without demands, manipulation, or struggle.

# Chapter Eight
## Flowing With Inspiration

Sometimes the result of being pushed toward the expectations of others relative to the pull of our true passions generates an undertow of internal conflict. When we are in alignment, the pulling force from which our guidance system extends its path is the target defined by our emotion of inspiration. When we live by what inspires us most and makes us feel alive, serendipitous connections and awareness of our internal and external resources increases. We recognize the abundance in our life and we think thoughts that mirror our value and inherent worthiness. The feeling of inspiration brings clarity and intention about who we are becoming, how we want to give, and what we want to do.

In the intentional creation of your life, if you do not currently know with very strong conviction what you need and want, prior to making any intellectual efforts to do so, I invite you to first dig deeper and into your more subtle knowing to determine how you want to feel. Intellectual evaluations are limited to what you already know and have experienced in the past, what you think is possible for you, and what you think others would like to see from you. Knowing how you want to feel will allow you to discover what you really want in your future. Shifting from a cerebral exploration to an emotional focus will also help you set goals accordingly so that you are inspired from within. Again, this is the energy that leads to effective action.

In the intentional creation of your life, and in considering your future goals, keep in mind that it is important to maintain a balanced perspective of life whereby you acknowledge that it is not one-sided. There will always be challenges, but these challenges are necessary for your growth. Without them, there would be no expansion and expansion is the purpose behind life itself. Furthermore, if you perceive that the future holds only support, you are simultaneously perceiving your current reality as having significantly more discomfort or dissatisfaction than benefits. From a resonance with assumed lack and unfelt appreciation for exactly what is, it can be extremely difficult to create change. Depression tends to be a byproduct of labeling your current situation as terrible, in a state of always resisting the present; rejecting and feeling dissatisfied at best and repulsed at worst, by what is.

Dynamic tension is the healthy degree of tension we experience when we are striving for something that is just outside our realm of experience, yet not beyond the degree of what we can perceive ourselves doing well. The tension threshold, as defined by behavioral scientists is a state of eustress. This form of stress actually improves performance, focuses, perseverance, clarity, and energy. It is this tension that moves us into growth and expansion. If we believe that our potential capability is equal to the challenge, we are right at the tension threshold. Productive tension can be stifled by negative stress — distress. Our neurochemistry transitions to the state of fight, flight, or freeze when we are believing that we do not have access to necessary external or internal resources to overcome our challenges at hand.

The more you recognize both your internal and external resources, the more you can maintain a state of eustress as you pursue your goals. Many of us have forgotten or have underestimated our two most important and most powerful inner resources — our unique type of intelligence and our ability to generate positive emotion by engaging in what inspires us most. This unawareness, in turn, causes us to become oblivious to our external resources. When we tap into our positive emotion, we suddenly awaken from our obliviousness of the abundance of resources available to us, which had likely always been here.

Society at large has led us to believe that inspiration is not important or that it should not necessarily be considered in any of your personal goals. This is detrimental to the progress of humanity. The force used to get people to participate in something they are not naturally curious about or do not find meaningful is externally applied motivation through reward and punishment. This is actually a thoroughly ineffective approach when innovation and creation are the desired outcomes.

Dan Pink, author of *Drive: The Surprising Truth About What Motivates Us*, among many other books, explains in his popular Ted Talk, The Puzzle of Motivation that research-supported science on both intrinsic and extrinsic human motivation proves that we accomplish significantly more when we are working toward a goal that we are inspired to achieve. When it comes to human effectiveness, multiple research experiments show us that intrinsic motivation maximizes conceptual problem-solving and creation, which are both the most important necessities for innovation. "If you want engagement, self-direction works better," Pink says. "Major companies such as Google and its employees engage this truth; for instance, roughly half of the new products they birthed were done during the allotted "free" time (20 percent of their overall workday hours) when they had autonomy over their task, team, and technique."

Dan Pink explains that it is not just speculation that the mechanistic reward-and-punishment approach you have likely been conforming to is actually ineffective and usually does harm. "Extensive studies conducted by economists from MIT sponsored by the Federal Reserve of the United States showed that when a task called for even rudimentary cognitive skill, a larger reward led to poorer performance," he writes, "because autonomy, mastery, and purpose are the platforms from which inspiration expresses itself." Innovation can be considered a state of inspired action, which is fueled by intrinsic motivation.

With certain elements in place, you experience a state of mind called flow that engages neurochemical and neuroanatomical expressions that significantly expedite learning and enhance performance. This term, flow, was coined by Dr. Mihaly Csikszentmihalyi, a professor of psychology whose research has proven that the most productive engagement of self involves your highest values. When your highest values and your innate strengths merge with your drive to create and contribute, you experience the state of flow. This state happens spontaneously as an intense focus brought forth from a perfect balance of inspiration along with a seeking of a solution to something (a challenge), and a certain degree of competency, known as your tension threshold.

A little dissatisfaction or desire for something else is needed, and the solution cannot extend beyond your perceived competence in order to enter into a state of flow. "If the balancing act of competence and challenge were to shift more into either above or beyond a specific degree of capability into either too capable or not yet ready, you would lose this state of mind," says Dr. Steven Kotler, who is an expert on the biology of flow and the author of *The Rise of Superman, Decoding the Science of Ultimate Human Performance*. Without this balance, you are more likely to enter into a state of apathy based on disinterest and distress due to being incapable of formulating a solution. Flow is a state of non-re-resistance.

In a Big Think interview, Dr. Kotler explains how certain biological reaction patterns present in the flow state augment the creative process by collectively enhancing pattern recognition and promoting lateral thinking. "Lateral thinking is required to link disparate things together," he says. "You can think of creativity as novel information sort of merging into old information to create something new or/and the linking of very disparate things together in unexpected but effective ways."

Dr. Kotler explains that a scientific research study had been done to induce flow artificially through stimulating activity in certain relevant neuroanatomical structures. As a result, 23 people solved a problem in record time that they had tried and failed miserably moments before the artificial stimulation. An additional experiment recorded that the neuro-feedback of marksmen who were practicing under this artificially induced flow learned 250 times faster than when they were engaged without artificially induced neuro-chemicals naturally produced in a state of flow. This turned the novice archers and marksmen into experts within half of the expected and average timeframe under normal neuro conditions. Essentially, these studies prove that flow offers the source code to massively amplify learning. Beyond the benefits of rapid learning, focused attention in and of itself also leads to greater happiness.

So, it is largely inspiration that stimulates the neurochemistry necessary to enter into a state of flow, and inspiration is driven by our values. Although we are not cognizant of them all, our brain is processing 1 billion bits of information every second. Not only do our past experiences influence our perception, but our values do as well. Therefore, our values hierarchy acts as the filter through which information is processed. It is a large part of what decides which 40 billion bits we are actually conscious of. This is made possible through a mechanism of the brain called the reticular activating system, or RAS; a group of cells at the base of our brain stem. These cells are responsible for sorting through the massive amounts of incoming information and bringing anything we find important to our attention including perceived threats and what is in alignment with your authentic desires. Our conscious awareness is dictated by the aspects that seek pleasure and avoid pain — our ego, of course.

We will forever be inclined to maintain a sense of safety and therefore make choices based upon our personal security, but the degree to which this is the case varies from person to person. Sometimes this difference can be felt as either wanting to escape a certain reality or wanting to create a certain reality. If you want to experience a change because it seems exciting or in alignment, you're right on track to creating it. If you are desperately seeking the avoidance of something, you will recreate that again and again. Which of these underlying motivations — avoidance of pain or seeking of pleasure — dominate our choices has much to do with our degree of self-esteem and self-efficacy. That is, our trust in our ability to figure things out, overcome challenges, and exhibit a positive orientation to life's struggles.

Meditation serves to strengthen self-efficacy and self-esteem. Through the practice of meditation we can begin to step outside of this habitual oscillation between avoidance and desperate seeking, which dictates most of our thoughts. Meditation slows the momentum of thought until the underlying eternal aspect of you that is not at all controlled by perceived threats and consists of only creative forces can come forth. This permanent underlying aspect of you is void of fear or seeking. It is simply felt as a vessel through which pure creation is allowed expression. You, in a sense, surrender to the universe and let it show you your assignment, calling, or purpose — what it is wanting to birth through you.

Your authentic hierarchy of values is the human expression of this creative force coming through your unique expression of your life. Your ego structure may assume values that you yourself never actually agreed to. In other words, your ego self may have taken on others' values as your own, but they are not birthed from your soul.

When you are pursuing goals that are not

resonant with your true values, you are actually working against yourself. This is because the functions of both your reticular activating system and your survival mechanism are causing you to see only either what is important to your physical survival or what resonates with your true values. Meanwhile, you are striving to see things that you think you should see in order to uphold the injected values and the various masks you've identified with and have placed upon figurative pedestals. This polarity causes incredible anxiety. Instead of acknowledging and pursuing our authentic values and instead of embracing meditation, our society is more inclined to take prescription drugs that drown out what is an inextricable part of our humanity.

Ultimately, neither the devaluing of ego and glorification of spirit, or the glorification of ego and devaluing of spirit offers a grounded and flourishing way of being in the world. We must work with certain aspects of the ego — like our desires, our roles, our aspirations, and our emotional fulfillment — and we must simultaneously be open to exploring the benefits of seemingly spiritual practices like meditation.

As we silence the mind and get in touch with the permanent infinite essence of existence itself, we automatically recognize that we are an extension of it. With this, things begin to dramatically shift in our inner world. We evolve through a series of self reflections whereby our understanding shifts from: things happen to me, to things happen from me, to things happen through me, to things happen as me. We evolve from the victim, to the creator, to the surrenderer, to realizing that we all are one with source. Until these realizations occur, our archaic wiring and primal existential fears that drive the illusion, make passive subjugation the only feasible option.

# Contribution: Competencies of Our Passions

Neuroscience shows us that when we are giving, the pleasure centers of our brain light up in a similar way to how they do in the state of flow. In many ways giving is an opportunity for connection. It connects us energetically with the heart whether or not the people involved in the exchange of energy actually ever meet. A brain-imaging study headed by neuroscientist Jordan Grafman from the National Institutes of Health discovered that the parts of the brain that are active when we experience pleasure are equally active when we both observe someone giving and when we are ourselves receiving. This study concluded that both giving and receiving were associated with heightened activity in regions of the midbrain that is known to be involved in primal desires, such as food and sex, and the satisfaction of them. "This result provides the first evidence that the 'joy of giving' has an anatomical basis in the brain – surprisingly, one that is shared with selfish longings and rewards," writes Daniel Stimson, Ph.D., in his online post Inner Workings of the Magnanimous Mind.

This is because the giver and the receiver are one in the same. When you willingly give; this exchange of energy is one and the same. The very moment it is given, it is received. It becomes of even greater significance, and the quality of our contribution is very high when it merges with our competencies and our passion. This emergence is that sweet spot of synergy among what we love to do (your highest value), what we are great at (or can be great at), and what people are in need of. When this combination is felt we automatically embrace our ultimate sense of purpose, and with this we perceive the world differently, so that our giving endures beyond the presence of our physical bodies.

*"Everybody is a genius. But if you judge a fish by its ability to climb a tree, it will live its whole life believing that it is stupid."* -- Albert Einstein

What often stagnates our flow and prevents out potential degree of contribution, and prevents us from embracing our authentic values is our indoctrination into an outdated and highly ineffective education system. There is so much human potential in the world that is not being tapped into because of the outdated assumptions and false definitions of intelligence that began being propagated in our school years.

There is almost nothing further from the truth that there are just a few types of intelligence and that if you do not do well within the standard assessments that support them, then you simply are unintelligent. "We all have a unique constellation of intelligence," says Ken Robinson, a prominent advocate for improving childhood education. The truth is that there exist multiple forms of intelligence and everyone embodies their own expression in ways that are unique to them. To paraphrase him, we all know that our school systems in the U.S. are based on conformity, not diversity, despite the fact that the nature of humanity is intrinsically diverse. They measure what kids can do across a very narrow spectrum of achievement.

Children thrive when we celebrate their various talents. When the right conditions present themselves the unique form of genius emerges. It is not that the intelligence is not there, it is simply in an unexpressed dormant state. Freedom of their authentic self is what would allow it to come forth into being and then utilized for the advantage of others and society. Robinson's research shows us that when students are energized via the engagement of curiosity, individuality and creativity, they excel — and this is no different for adults. Robinson states that if we live from our unique "element", as he put it, we decrease the default state of conformity and become more courageous and self-reliant.

Allow me to illustrate a few examples of the multiple forms of intelligences that are not acknowledged in education systems and within any form of standardized education-related assessments. In Liberating Everyday Genius, Dr. Mary-Elaine Jacobsen, a doctor of psychology,  states that "Giftedness is not merely as giftedness does or how it thinks, it is also as it feels, senses, and perceives." She has identified an evolutionary intelligence, which is indicative of an ability to thrive in dynamic environments while expanding the collective knowledge base. She writes: "I cannot think of a more dynamic expression than that of humanity and nature itself. Those who exemplify this type of intelligence can detect and define problems and envision creative solutions. It is at once outwardly focused and inwardly inspired, both visionary and pragmatic." This formula comprises the presence of talents and drive, and advanced development of humanistic vision, mission, and revolutionary action. This potential is undermined when authenticity is suppressed, conformity is insisted upon, and the underlying expectation that this is supposed to stimulate learning and growth.

Tojo Thatchenkery and Carol Metzker, authors of Appreciative Intelligence, draw upon their original research and recent discoveries in psychology and cognitive neuroscience to uncover the characteristics they conceive as appreciative intelligence — that is, the ability behind creativity, leadership, and success. The attributes of people with this type of intelligence are realistic and action-oriented, meaning they have the ability not just to identify positive potential, but also to devise a course of action to take advantage of it. In simpler terms, they are optimistic.

Research findings indicate that optimists are more successful than pessimists. While pessimists are realists — which can be a very good thing — they tend to lack the inspired action and passion that is the driving force behind the success of optimists. This is because of what is defined as a self-fulfilling prophecy. For instance, pessimists see the reality of their performance, and optimists perceive it as better than it may have actually been. As a result, optimists are more likely to do it repeatedly to establish a practice pattern that does ultimately end in great performance. They can see potential where it does not yet exist in form and seems to be impossible and have a very strong degree of persistence, a conviction that their actions matter, tolerance for uncertainty, and irrepressible resilience.

Speaking of optimism, if you think about it, the quality of your life is directly correlated to the quality of emotions you feel on a daily basis. It is such a blessing that humans are equipped with the ability to actually generate positive emotions. With persistent practice, shifting your orientation to see the positive in daily experiences eventually becomes habitual. Although, this can only be possible if your general underlying assumption about yourself is positive.

We are constantly under the influence of who we think and feel that we are; whether this is subtle or obvious, it is nevertheless always present. When the assumption is positive, you have leverage that makes it possible to intentionally shift into positive emotional states. Again, this is one reason why the inner work of emotional healing designed to shift your self-perception is so fundamental to your spiritual journey and for living out your purpose. When your underlying emotional state (electromagnetic vibration) is slanted toward the positive you can contribute to others. If it is negative, bitterness, apathy, and anger prevents your ability to contribute and serve.

There is a domino effect that happens when there are, even very subtle, shifts in positive emotion. Positive emotion eventually leads to both a heightened recognition of resources in ourselves (and our environment) and measurable improvements in well-being that have lasting effects. Essentially, positive emotion leads to the highest and best interpretation of external occurrences relative to our own personal desires and potential. This is why when we are feeling authentically good we make decisions that benefit our well-being and produce positive outcomes.

Dr. Barbara Lee Fredrickson is a social psychologist who conducts research on emotions and positive psychology. She is also the author of *Positivity*, a general-audience book that draws on her own research and that of other social scientists. Her main work is related to her broaden-and-build theory of positive emotions. This theory emphasizes the fact that positive emotions lead to novel, expansive or exploratory behavior, and over time, these actions lead to meaningful, long-term resources such as knowledge and social relationships.

She coined the phrase "positivity offset" and argues that even though positive experiences generally occur more frequently, negative ones have greater weight and tend to linger. Even if positive emotions are present, you usually view them as neutral. Optimism requires intentional effort due to this positivity offset. Fortunately, you can become aware of them and choose to use them in a way that naturally leads to an upward emotional spiral. That is, because positive emotions tend to be subtler than negative emotions you have to pay more attention to the goodness in your life. In addition to cultivating and intentionally integrating more positive experiences into your life, simply being more cognizant of your emotional states is influential. This awareness leads to a higher ratio of positive-to-negative emotions on average.

There are 10 positive emotions that we can choose to savor more. In doing so, each offers a byproduct that further stimulates happiness and personal expansion. Consider these examples: joy stimulates playfulness, which then evokes more joy; savoring serenity causes peace of mind; interest stimulates exploration, and the outcome is knowledge; pride is achievement that causes people to dream bigger, leading to more achievements; amusement generates shared laughter and connections; inspiration happens most when we witness human excellence and this inspires our own desire for excellence; and awe is the feeling of being overwhelmed by greatness or grandness. Each of these examples allows us to see ourselves as part of a larger whole and emphasizes the desire to fulfill our spiritual needs — contribution, connection, and growth.

Inclusive to engaging in the Arete Process I suggest you start a ritual of journal exercises in which you list all of the ways you experienced any of the positive emotions detailed in this chapter and how they resulted in even more positivity in your day. I also recommend that you read Hal Elrod's book, The Miracle Morning, and apply the morning rituals he teaches. These are wonderful habits for improving your wellbeing. Incorporating a focus upon your daily positive emotional experiences into Hal's series of five powerful morning practices — silence, affirmations, visualization, exercise, and reading — is my highest suggestion for actively generating positive emotion more readily in you life.

# *In Closing*

In Plato's Republic, Socrates describes a group of people who lived chained in a cave for all their lives facing a blank wall. All they could see were shadows projected on the wall by things passing by in front of a fire, which was behind them. This puppet show became their world. According to Socrates, the shadows were the closest they'd ever get to seeing reality. Even if they suspected there was more, they were unwilling to leave what was familiar.

Oftentimes spiritual and self-help practices are likened to manipulating the shadows on the cave wall so as to cope with life more efficiently, nevertheless you are still reconfiguring only the shadows. What you are modifying is not real. Most people are content here and even knowing this, which is absolutely fine, of course. Others may feel called to see the truth of all existence as opposed to the shadows, the illusions.

In considering the metaphorical chains I mentioned at the beginning of this book; the ones that you assume are holding you back. It is only after the acknowledgment of and respect for the influential aspects of your shadow, can you then realize that the chains are all an illusion. We must turn our attention away from the shadows and toward the light if we are going to see the truth, but if one is too accustomed to the darkness, they must gradually become accustomed to the light. Your old identity must die to new growth. This is transformation.

The truth of who you are is simply buried deep within your being. Transformation is allowing your authenticity to come forth. Deep self-awareness is the only thing required for you to see what is or isn't already here. You will soon discover that while the shadow is the cause of your struggle, this realization offers your liberation from it.

I hope that this book inspires you to move forward with full appreciation for your life and of life itself. May you share your authenticity with joy and peace in your heart and with full gratitude for your gifts. May you continue your life in pure appreciation for your unique biological expression of infinite possibilities and that of others in your life.

As Reverend Michael Beckwith, founder of the Agape International Spiritual Center, reminds us that gratitude opens every door. In fact, the doors have always been open, it has just been our perception of unworthiness and misdirected focus upon what is lacking instead of focus upon the presence of abundance that is, that has caused them to appear close. Live in pure appreciation, and you will enter heaven on earth. The password that opens every door is, *Thank You*.

Lastly, may you always ask how can you find

purpose and growth behind your challenges. Relatively few people just drift into meaningful advancements and fulfillment; often it is the storms that activate latent potential within us. Simply acknowledging that the obstacle can be the very thing that catalyzes your growth is powerful, but when it is growth toward the accomplishment of your highest value, the effect is tremendous.

Just like how the specific molecules of an onion that makes you cry is the most nutritious component of the entire onion, our challenges — the ones that make us cry — can ultimately offer us the most value. For some of us, our calling is forged from overcoming our greatest challenges. Our narrative is often woven into our purpose because there is a direct emotional understanding and connection with those who are experiencing what we had experienced. This emotional resonance, as well as our personal evidence of the alternative to their pain, can contribute to our success and fulfillment.

Each of my struggles makes for the context of this book in addition to it being the direct conduit for my deepest healing. I am therefore, grateful for all that brought me to this point; to my calling and my destiny. I wish you the same.

"Take poison and make it into medicine." — Buddha

# <u>INSPIRING QUOTES</u>

"When the body (feelings) are controlling your interpretations of reality, you are not the master of your fate." - Dr. Joe Dispenza.

"It is as if the pain becomes fuel for the flame of your consciousness which then burns more brightly as a result." - Eckhart Tolle

"No person is free who is not master of himself." - Epictetus

"The happiest among us are the ones who have found a way to give ourselves away." – Unknown

"When the voice on the inside is louder than all voices and opinions on the outside is when we have begun to master our lives." - Dr. John Demartini.

" Vitality is directly proportionate to the vividness of your vision" - Dr. Demartini

"As long as getting dominates our intentions, our personal power is in a state of paralysis." – Bob Proctor

"We do not sing because we are happy, we are happy because we sing." - William James

"All of life is an experiment, therefore be willing to make more mistakes." - Ralph Emerson

"It is a fact that our implicit assumptions about our future powerfully affects our motivation. A person's image of the future may be a better predictor of future attainment than his past performance. " - Alfred Bandera

"Happiness, health, and prosperity are a result of a harmonious adjustment of the inner with the outer. Suffering is always the result of wrong thought. It is an indication of the individual out of harmony with himself and the law of his being." - Emerson

"Every human has a natural inclination to ascend to higher planes of existence, but it rests upon each of us to match that inclination with real initiative. Seeking to ascend in life takes grit and resolve, struggle and courage. But to those who make the effort belong all the glories of life. A vibrant, genuine, and purposeful life is the right of all humankind, but most of us fail to grasp it. "-

"The cave you fear to enter holds the treasure you seek." - Joseph Campbell

"Fear and pain should be treated as signals not to close our eyes but to open them wider." - Nathaniel Branden

"Paramount should be your concern to be aware of the values that move and guide you, as well as the roots, so that you are not ruled by values you have irrationally adopted or unknowingly accepted from others. One of the forms that living unconsciously takes is the obliviousness to the values guiding one's actions and even the indifference to the question." - Nathaniel Branden

"We become our true selves to the degree we make everyone else ourselves." - Schopenhauer

"The seer, the seeing, and the seen are always the same." - Aristotle

"Do not fear mistakes, jump in and hope to learn enough to correct them eventually. Freedom comes from embracing this truth and allowing life to be an experiment. When we fully accept ourselves is when we are willing to fail because our entire being is not on the line."- Maslow

"Ask yourself, what is my inner relationship with the present moment? Am I friendly or am I hostile

to it? The present moment is all you ever have. To treat this moment as if it were an obstacle to where you want to get to is the source of your obstacles. Inner peace is a much more powerful foundation for right action than resistance. Then see how your world changes as you no longer resist this moment."
- Eckhart Tolle

"When we are no longer able to change a situation we are challenged to change ourselves" - Victor Frank

## ACKNOWLEDGMENTS

A special thanks to my husband, Paulo Bertholdo, for supporting me through the creation of this book. To my mom for being the catalyst that forced my growth. My friends, Jennifer Lawrence, Dana Malstaff, Nahied Rahimi, Audrey Jacobs, Leah Kent, and Annette Chacon for always being there for me. For my entire amazing, wonderful, magnificent, beautiful Anzaldua family!

## About the Author

Lisa Marie Anzaldua is a transformation coach, an interior designer, author, wife and mother of two boys. Lisa Marie studied interior design with the Art Institute of California-San Francisco and earned a design degree and certification at West Valley College in Northern California. Additionally, she holds a degree in liberal arts with an emphasis in art history, and a business administration degree.

## WORKS CITED

Ted Talks. "Ken Robinson: Do Schools Kill Creativity." Online video clip. Ted Talks, February 2006. Web. 15 March 2016.

Ted Talks. "Dan Pink: The Puzzle of Motivation." Online video clip. Ted Talks, July 2009. Web. 08 November 2015.

Ted Talks. "Amy Cuddy: Your Body Language Shapes Who You Are." Online video clip. Ted Talks, June 2012. Web. 08 February 2016.

Demartini, Dr. John. "DrDemartini.com." Demartini 2007. Web. 01 January 2016.

Thatchenkery, Tojo PH.D. & Metzger, Carol. Appreciative Intelligence. San Francisco, California: Berrett-Koehler Publishers, 2006.

Rath, Tom. Strengths Finder 2.0. City and state: Gallup Press, 2013

Teal Swan. "Endurism (The Flip Side of Escapism)." Online video clip. YouTube, April 2016. Web. 01 May 2016.

Teal Swan. "I Can Have Me and I Can Have You Too." Online video clip. YouTube, May 2016. Web. 01 May 2016.

Bentinho Massaro. "The Seven Densities Explained". Online video clip. YouTube, September 2015. Web. 26 February 2016.

Bentinho Massaro. "Realize Infinite Self Love (Die Before You Die)". Online video clip. YouTube, May 2015. Web. 26 January 2016.

Travis Eric. "Bentinho Massaro - Choose Your Next Feeling". Online video clip. YouTube, January 2016. Web. 26 January 2016.

Dr. Dispenza, Joe. Breaking the Habit of Being Yourself: How to Lose Your Mind and Create a

New One. Carlsbad, California: Hay House, Inc., 2012.

P.H. D. Stimson, Daniel. "Inner Workings of the Magnanimous Mind." The National Institute of Neurological Disorders, n.p. 04 April 2007. Web. 12 May 2016.

Seppala, Emma. "The Compassionate Mind: Science Shows Why it's Healthy and How it Spreads" Association for Psychological Science, Observer Vol.26, No.5 May/June, 2013. Web. 05 May 2016.

Burchard, Brendon. The Charge: Activating the 10 Human Drives That Make You Feel Alive. New York, New York: Free Press, 2012.

Robbins, Tony. Awaken the Giant Within: How to Take Immediate Control of Your Mental, Emotional, Physical and Financial Destiny. New York, New York: Free Press, 1991.

Dr. Maltz, Maxwell. Psycho-Cybernetics. New York, New York: Penguin Random House, 2015.

Elrod, Hal. The Miracle Morning. Hal Elrod International, 2014

Ted Talks. "Kelly McGonigal: How to Make Stress Your Friend." Online video clip. Ted Talks, June 2013. Web. 08 February 2016.

Keller, Gary & Papasan, Jay. The One Thing: The Simple Truth Behind Extraordinary Results. Austin, TX: Bard Press, 2013.